Katheri

TO THE
ABYSS

You give me hope!

Thank you ♥

RP

TO THE
ABYSS

RACHEL N. PAVERMAN

PALMETTO
PUBLISHING

Charleston, SC
www.PalmettoPublishing.com

To The Abyss

Copyright © 2022 by Rachel N. Paverman

First Edition

Paperback ISBN: 978-1-68515-899-6
eBook ISBN: 978-1-68515-900-9

In Loving Memory of Lauren Marie Brescia
a shining light when everything was dark
thank you for coming into my life
1983-2021

TABLE OF CONTENTS

CHAPTER 1

My journey has been a roller coaster, so I'd like to take you back to the very beginning of this long and crazy story that I like to call life. I was born a normal, healthy child on July 29, 1994 in New Brunswick, NJ. I have two amazing parents named Alan and Stacey and an older sister, Rebecca. She is three years older than I am and we have always been extremely close. I grew up pretty comfortably in Manalapan, New Jersey on a quiet street where all of the neighborhood kids spent their time playing outdoors and enjoying the fresh air year round.

You name it, we did it- swimming, playing on the swing sets, jumping on the trampoline, lemonade stands, catching lightning bugs, playing manhunt, ordering all of the Spice Girls lollipops from the ice cream truck. And then during the winter we would build igloos, sled down the big hill in our neighbor Richie's backyard, have snowball fights. The best memory that I have of winters in Manalapan is when my dad used to tie our dog Ginger's leash to the handle of our sled. Ginger would sprint down the long and slushy street, pulling us one at a time on the sled. Ginger Spice (a yellow lab that was named after one of the

Spice Girls) loved the snow!! She would always try biting it as it fell from the sky. Can you tell that my sister and I liked the Spice Girls growing up though?

I played soccer for as long as I can remember. My dad was always the coach of my team. I loved soccer so much. I always looked forward to the weekends because I had a game every Sunday. I was the goal scorer and I loved every bit of those years. I had a pretty damn good childhood, and some amazing memories growing up.

As I was growing up though, I remember that my parents weren't the two happy parents in love that I'd see on the tv. When they weren't fighting with each other, they just weren't talking to each other. They just co-existed. I don't remember them ever sleeping in the same room. The only time that my sister and I would have a babysitter was when my parents were attending a wedding or a special event. They never went out just to go on dates. My poor, poor babysitter though. I was literally a terror. I would give her such a hard time, especially when it was bedtime. My sister would pretend that she was going to sleep too and then once I was asleep, Rebecca would quietly emerge from her room to stay up later with the babysitter. I was such a little shit. My mom always made a joke that if I was the first born child, I'd be an only child. What can I say- I was a rebellious kid. Sorry to all those that I tortured as a child- I swear I didn't mean it.

When I was twelve years old, my parents filed for their divorce. Although my sister and I knew that they had disagreements, we never thought that they would actually split up. We didn't know what real love looked like, but just assumed that their twisted relationship was normal because we didn't know any better. I remember overhearing a conversation between my parents once discussing details of their divorce before they actually told us that they were getting a divorce. I went straight to Rebecca with what I overheard. "Don't be silly, Rach. They are fine. That's not true."

A couple of days later, our twelve and fifteen year old lives were turned upside down. Mom and dad sat my sister and I down to tell us that they were getting a divorce, we were moving to a new town, and I'd have to start at a new school mid-year, at twelve years old. In 2007, I moved to a townhouse with my mom and my sister where we began living our new normal. It was really nice because my dad moved ten minutes away, so we would see him on the weekends, and occasionally during the week too. Soon after we adjusted to our new life, my mom was set up on a blind date that luckily introduced her to the man that's been in more than half of my life, Mike. I'm not going to lie, I was a real bitch to him at first. What do you expect from a hormonal pre-teen who had just been thrown into a new house, new school, and now a new boyfriend that my mother was dating. It wasn't him, it was the shitty situation that I had a tough time dealing with. I honestly love Mike so much! He is so important to me and I am extremely grateful for him. He has taught me so much about life and I appreciate that man beyond measure. He is like a second father to me.

Starting at a new school in the middle of my tween years was rough for me. I had to make new friends, I had new teachers. Not one familiar face that I knew. It wasn't fun being the "new girl" at school. I hated having attention on me. On top of the big changes that were happening in my life, that's when I started to feel like something was "off" in my body. I guess you could call that stress, but to me, it was something that needed to be addressed. I longed for answers as to why I always felt fatigued, nauseous, dizzy and my brain felt foggy. I was told that it was just my anxiety and stress from my current life situation, but I didn't believe it. My mom brought me to multiple specialists until finally, we got an answer from a pediatric endocrinologist. She said that I had Polycystic Ovarian Syndrome (PCOS) and hypothyroidism.

That was the answer I was given for my many odd symptoms. It was weird to me that I was diagnosed with PCOS, because I was right at the peak of my hormones, and I wasn't overweight which was common with PCOS. I was a little twig. The doctor prescribed me two drugs that I was taking for a couple of weeks before I started getting extremely sick.

I had a rapid heartbeat, heart palpitations and more dizziness than before which landed me in the emergency room. At that point, we opted for an additional opinion to see if there was any other medication options that could help me. My new doctor's words were the first time that I heard this phrase, but definitely not the last time. "Well, you're sort of in the 'gray area'," she said, "The numbers that came back from your blood test are slightly off, but it doesn't fully indicate to me that you have hypothyroidism or PCOS".

After that appointment, I stopped taking the two prescriptions all together, still longing for answers as to why I felt the way that I did- just not right. Not myself. The new doctor prescribed me birth control to regulate my hormones, since they were all wacky, plus my period was super irregular. It helped a little, and I was able to get by with minimized symptoms.

I started high school in 2008. I really enjoyed art and I loved using my creativity to make it, specifically mosaics and drawing. I was very active- I played field hockey and lacrosse for the school, and soccer for the town where I grew up. I had a really great high school experience. In my senior year, I met Brandon. He went to a nearby Catholic school, and we met each other through our mutual friends. I was so in love with that boy from the minute that I met him. We were inseparable. I had a bunch of little relationships throughout high school that really only lasted a couple of months because I was so picky and would always find a reason not to like them anymore. With Brandon, it was different. He was like the boy version of me. We got along so well right from the beginning of our relationship. I was infatuated and totally head over heels for Bran.

I committed to Montclair State University for fall of 2012, and life was really great. Not a responsibility or care in the world. I had a bunch of friends, partied a lot aka drank every weekend until I basically blacked out, smoked a stupid amount of weed-reckless and dumb teenager stuff. Every weekend that my mom was away was my chance to throw a house party and let anyone random in my house. I look back at that now and cringe at the stupidity. Rebecca, my sister, was the golden child, and I was the absolute train wreck. I would get grounded all of the time and get my phone or computer taken away from me. I thought that I was the shit and completely invincible.

The summer before college after my senior year was supposed to be a fun time, one last hoorah if you will, but it took a turn for me. I remember the exact day I started to feel like something was "off" again.

CHAPTER 2

I was a cashier at the local grocery store, working the night shift. My two friends were waiting outside to pick me up after my shift ended and we were planning to head down to Seaside Heights on the Jersey Shore. It was Brandon's nineteenth birthday and his friends booked a couple of rooms at some sketchy motel where we were all planning to get wasted and party.

Before my shift ended at work that night, I started to get that feeling again where I got randomly super dizzy and I was very nauseous. This time around, the nausea that I had was more severe. It would come in waves. It felt like I was going to be sick but I never actually got sick. I bought some ginger ale, tums and pepto before my shift ended and I was able to ignore the miserable feeling for the night.

Weeks and weeks passed by with the same gross feeling, plus now I had aches throughout my neck and shoulders. It felt like I was getting arthritis. At that point, my parents and I decided that we'd go to specialists for every symptom that I acquired, trying to pinpoint a cause for it all. We didn't know how to tackle it. First on the list? Gastroenterologist to address the nausea and stomach aches. My doctor ordered the first of many colonoscopies and endoscopies as well as some blood work. After just one colonoscopy, we had our answer. "You definitely have a form of Crohn's disease. You also have fibromyalgia, which explains the uncomfortable aches you've been feeling."

This isn't the kind of news that an 18-year-old girl wanted to hear the summer before she headed off to college but I guess that it gave me all of the answers that I was seeking. Crohn's disease is a chronic inflammatory disease that affects the lining of the digestive tract. Fibromyalgia is muscle pain and tenderness with fatigue that can alter sleep, memory, and mood. "You're going to start a medication regimen for Crohn's disease and see how that helps you. Unfortunately, there's nothing that can be done for fibromyalgia though. I suggest applying heat when you have a flare up."

If you know me, you'd know that I'm not very big on taking medicine because I feel like it's putting chemicals in your body that aren't supposed to be there. Our ancestors got by just fine without taking any medication, so why did we need it? I didn't even like to take Tylenol if I didn't have to. I was desperate to feel better though, especially before heading off for my first year of college. I followed the instructions given to me by my doctor, and took the medicine throughout my first fall semester at school.

I was still getting really sick and the medication didn't seem to be helping me. I went from 128 pounds down to almost about 100 pounds. I looked so sickly thin. I really couldn't eat much but when I did eat, I would get sick afterwards...it probably didn't help that I was stuck eating college cafeteria food everyday though. I was being patient with the medication but it didn't seem to be helping me much, if at all.

That January, when I was home for winter break, my doctor prescribed a stronger medication that was way more intense. It was a self-injectable pen with a lot more potential long-term side effects. Once I was back at school, my dad had to drive up every two weeks to deliver new pens for me to stick in my thigh or belly. The pens had to be stored at a cool temperature so he brought them up in a cooler. I was storing all of my medication in my dorm room mini fridge while all of the other kids were storing beer in theirs.

I would inject the pen once a week in either my thigh or belly. On the days when I administered the injection, I felt horrible. I would curl into a ball all day in my bed. I had body aches and major fatigue- I remember not making it to class on some of those days. I stopped drinking alcohol because feeling sick wasn't worth it to me. But, I wanted to give the medicine time to work in my body. After all, I had Crohn's and I needed something to help me. I was eventually put on disability at school which meant that housing allowed me to have a single dorm room. I felt crappy and it made things worse when I'd have a roommate stumbling in the room at 3 AM and wake me up. The medication seemed to work some of the time, but not all the time, and the side effects from it really weren't worth it to me. After about two years of back and forth medicine drop offs to doctors visits, we decided to see a different doctor. Maybe he would have another suggestion for me to control my constant Crohn's flare ups.

After ordering blood work and a colonoscopy, he seemed to have a drastically different opinion. The same phrase was said to me, "You're in the 'gray area'. To be completely honest, I'm questioning if you even have Crohn's disease or fibromyalgia. I think you might just have a bad case of IBS. We'll just give you medication to manage your symptoms as they come."

You would think that hearing this would be amazing news and I would be ecstatic to hear that things were okay in my body. The truth is, I was devastated. Devastated to hear that I had put so much trust in my doctor again and was completely let down. Devastated that I had been giving myself medication or should I say "chemicals" for two years that I didn't even need apparently. On the contrary, I was very happy to hear that I was okay and this would not debilitate me for my entire life. It was really embarrassing for me to now explain to my family and friends that I was actually fine- no Crohn's for me. Just kidding everyone, it's actually nothing!

My new doctor told me that he would be doing colonoscopy check ups every three months or so to make sure that things stabilized in my colon. After a few more clear colonoscopies, my doctor found something concerning on my colon. He biopsied a polyp that turned out to be precancerous. He was luckily able to remove the whole thing though. I couldn't help but think that this growth was because of all the injections that I was giving to myself for two years prior. He told me that if this polyp wasn't detected or removed when he had removed it, it would have eventually turned into full blown cancer in my colon.

I just kept feeling defeated- like I would finally solve the mystery of what the hell was going on with my body and then a doctor would say "nope, sike. Still a mystery babe." I felt like people didn't believe me anymore. I even started to convince myself that I was making it all up. I didn't drink. Nobody ever said anything to me about that, but I knew that people thought it was kind of weird that I didn't drink- like I was a buzzkill or something. Drinking was a way for people to be social with each other. It was even more awkward when friends would buy rounds of shots at the bar and I would have to reject it politely.

Whenever I tried to drink even just a little bit, I would feel dizzy and get intense waves of nausea- drinking wasn't worth that to me in all honesty. I put my focus and energy towards my health, working out, and discovering what I had interest in. I had to figure out what I wanted to major in since I started college without a major. I took a general education class in marketing and loved that. There was a major at my school called Sports, Events and Tourism Marketing. I figured that I loved playing sports my whole life, enjoyed watching sports, and thought that event planning sounded glam, so I decided to declare that as my major. Sports, Events and Tourism Marketing. I set a goal for myself from that day on that I would try to make connections with as many people in the industry as I could and learn from them. Networking was the best tool for learning. I was ten minutes down the road from the New York Giants facility and MetLife Stadium, and 25 minutes away from New York City; I just had to get my foot in the door somewhere.

In my junior year of college, a guest speaker came to my sports marketing class to talk about the business world of sports. Ethan was the director of Partnerships at the time for the New York Giants. His lecture was so interesting and validated even further why I picked the right major for me. I made sure that I stayed after class to talk to him and pick his brain about how he got to where he was in his career. Ethan gave me his business card and told me that I could reach out to him anytime with questions.

A couple of weeks later, my friend got me a gig at MetLife stadium where I would help to promote different brands that were partnered with the stadium on game days. I ran into Ethan often when the Giants played, and stayed in touch with him the rest of that school year. I look at Ethan as a mentor and a friend. He is really great at his job and I have so much respect for him- he's a genuinely wonderful person and just wanted to teach me how to be successful and help me flourish in my young career. I honestly owe the development of my sports career to Ethan. He really helped me. Right before graduation senior year, Ethan helped me get an interview for a temporary position with the Premium Services Department at the New York Giants.

I got along so well with the director there, so I landed the job, planning to begin in July of 2016, right before training camp of the 2016 season started. I also worked all of the game days from 2017-2019. This also led me to the opportunity to work for the NFL at Super Bowl LI in Houston, Texas. I worked on their communications team. I managed the media for the weeks leading up to the Super Bowl and at the actual Super Bowl, managed press conferences with Lady Gaga, Commissioner Goodell, both respective teams and key players, etc. The experience was awesome and a one of a kind opportunity.

WORKING SUPER BOWL 51 IN HOUSTON, TX

After that, I got a job where I was a youth football events coordinator. I traveled all over the country- Arizona, California, Colorado, Nevada, Missouri, Texas, Florida, Ohio. It seemed like some of the health issues that I was experiencing had totally just melted away. The fatigue, though? That definitely never melted away for me. I would get so tired that the glands in my neck would pop out. The nausea didn't melt away either which is why I always carried anti-nausea meds and a water bottle with me everywhere I went.

The most recent job I had was with the largest medical communications company in the USA where I was an events and meeting planner. I basically organized and planned conferences for oncologists that were looking to attend educational programs to obtain CME credits for their medical licenses, and I traveled… A LOT! Some of the cool places work had brought me were Miami Beach, Barcelona, Huntington Beach, Chicago, Atlanta, Hawaii, Las Vegas, Houston, San Antonio- the list goes on!

I was promoted to a new role in May of 2019 where I planned advisory boards at these large conferences. Advisory boards were small, round table discussions for physicians that were usually funded by pharmaceutical companies. Oncologists would watch presentations, usually over dinner and drinks and discuss a specific drug treatment that was being offered by the pharmaceutical company hosting the program. It was my job to track and plan all flights and ground transportation for the physicians, order and oversee the audio visual techs, make sure that the content was recorded and the room was set up correctly, order all food and beverage for the program, and make sure that it was brought out at the right time. There's also a million other little things that I would do too. Ask anyone on my team, as an event planner, any issue on site becomes your issue to figure out.

Although it was stressful, I loved my job- it was so rewarding to know that I was part of the education that oncologists were receiving. They could use all of the information given to them at the conferences that I planned to help their patients heal. Life was good. I was living with my boyfriend, Brandon, traveling to amazing places, and loved my job despite all of the stress it gave me, especially after my recent promotion. In June of 2019 though, my health took a turn… yet again. I remember exactly when this happened.

CHAPTER 3

Brandon was in Boston for the week for work and I was home, holding down the fort. It was the weekend. I cleaned the house, went to the gym, and just relaxed on Saturday evening, catching up on the Bachelor. On Sunday morning, I woke up and was having trouble swallowing the water that was on my nightstand. I could do it, but I had to think about the act of swallowing to actually get a sip down. I convinced myself it was just my anxiety making me crazy, and the stress from my new promotion at work just getting to me. After all, I'd been seen by plenty of doctors who told me that I was fine.

Over the course of the week that Brandon was gone, it went from having to think about swallowing liquids, to only being able to drink ice cold liquids through a straw. Even then, I had to think about every sip that I took in order to be able to swallow it. There were a few times that water would slip down my throat without me swallowing it which would make me cough. I told my family about this weird new sensation that I was having but they all validated my thought that it was stress and anxiety. I met my sister at Jersey Freeze for a milkshake that week. The sensation was even difficult when I drank a thick milkshake. Over the next two months, other strange things happened. I would occasionally drool when I was laying in bed at night but Brandon and I would just laugh it off.

Then, at kickboxing one day, I wasn't able to drink my water after a hard workout when I was dying of thirst. Another day, at work, I walked up to my co-worker's desk to ask her a question and burst out laughing for no reason. I was literally in tears, uncontrollably laughing, and nothing was even remotely funny- it was so embarrassing. Another time over this two month period, I was sitting at the bar with Brandon one night. I got a dizzy spell that was so severe that I had to grab onto the bar top and squeeze my eyes shut because the room was spinning and I thought that I was going to fall off of my bar stool. It only lasted for a couple of seconds, but it was so intense.

I also started to notice that I wasn't holding my pen as tight anymore, or applying my eyeliner with a steady grasp. Everytime I thought that something was wrong in the past though, I was shut down by a medical professional who told me that I was fine. I started seeing a therapist since it was hammered into my brain that I had stress and anxiety which was causing these random medical issues. I'm not going to lie, my anxiety was off the charts lately too. I was literally starting to become afraid to drive thirty minutes home after work each day, a drive that I took everyday for two years. I decided to see my primary care doctor also. She too suggested it might be from my anxiety and high stress.

However, she wanted to rule things out so she ordered an ultrasound of my thyroid to see if something might be on my thyroid that would prevent me from swallowing correctly. That scan came back crystal clear. I started looking up some of the symptoms that I was experiencing and tried piecing things together on my own. I was convinced that I had Multiple Sclerosis, ALS, or another type of neurological condition. I confided in one of my closest friends at work during lunch that day and just started crying to her. My emotions were a mess and I wasn't able to control them, whether it was crying or laughing. That night, I went on my computer and took it into my own hands to research a local neurologist.

After two long weeks of waiting for my initial consultation, I had my appointment. My mom knew that I was very nervous about it so she met me there. After a complete physical exam by the neurologist, he said that I passed all of the neurological tests with flying colors. "Uhhhh, OK? And? Now what?" I thought. I know that I should have been very happy and relieved with the positive news, but I again just felt defeated by the medical field. No one believed me but something was definitely wrong with me! I wasn't crazy. I just didn't feel right. "I'm going to order an MRI just so we can be sure, though." The MRI had to be authorized by my insurance company which took about a week. After it got approved, I was thinking about not even getting the MRI done.

A- It was going to be expensive.

B- He didn't see anything wrong with me during my physical exam, so why should I even bother wasting the money and time if it was just going to come back normal?

I don't know what it was, but something in me decided to call and schedule an MRI despite the cost and inconvenience. I wanted to schedule a day where I knew that I could work from home and get it done during my lunch break. Thursday, September 19 was the date that was available. Little did I know this date would change my life forever.

CHAPTER 4

During the week of September 9, 2019, I was in Washington D.C. running a large conference for work. On the weekend of September 14, 2019, I was at my beach house with my friends. We went out to Atlantic City and spent the next day on the beach. On Monday, September 16, 2019, I attended the Monday night football game. It was the New York Jets versus the Cleveland Browns. I went after work with my dad. We are Giants fans, but my uncle gave us free tickets to go plus it was the first year that Odell Beckham Jr. was traded to the Browns so we had to go to see him!

Waking up on Thursday, September 19, 2019 was just like any normal morning when I was working from home. I was up by 7:00 AM, went to the drive thru for some iced coffee and a breakfast sammy, and was on my computer by 8:00 AM. Emails had flooded my inbox from the night before and I spent the morning sifting through them.

I liked working from home. I turned our second bedroom into a home office; I bought a desk on Amazon and put it together all by myself. I set up a second computer monitor too. When

I worked at home, I always got more work done because I could be totally focused and uninterrupted. When I was at the office, it was distracting because my friends sat in the cubicles next to me, I'd have meetings all day, or my phone would be ringing off the hook. The day would just get away from me and before I knew it, it would be 5:30 PM.

I had two programs coming up that I was working on. One was in Boston, Massachusetts (a smaller round table program) and the other one was in Atlantic City, NJ, which was a huge conference with thousands of attendees. I was home, I could focus, and I had my to-do list for the day with some big bucket items that I wanted to complete. Time flies when you are busy though and before I knew it, it was 12:00 PM. I had to get going in a couple of minutes to make my 12:30 PM MRI.

Oftentimes when I had a lot to do, I would just work through my lunch hour. I wished that I could have done that. I told myself that I would just work a little after 5:30 PM to make sure that I could complete the stuff that I wanted to complete. I got into my car and drove to the radiology center, which was about ten minutes away from my house. The parking lot was pretty packed, but I managed to find a spot in the lot that faced the main road. I put my car in park, flipped down the mirror, put on some chapstick and walked into the building. Little did I know, that would be the last time I'd drive a car for a very long time.

The building was very big and had a lot of medical offices within it. I had to walk all the way to the end of the hallway until I found the radiology office. I checked in, but it was packed with people. "Great, this is going to take forever," I thought. After about a twenty minute wait (not so bad), a bald, tall man with tattoos on his arms called my name. He brought me to a tiny room where I could keep my belongings, and he handed me a gown to change into. The room was basically a closet with a bench, locker and curtain. "Here, put this on. Make sure you take off all jewelry too. No metal in the MRI machine," and shut the curtain so that I could change.

After I took off my necklace, earrings, and put the gown on, I drew the curtain open to walk to the MRI room across the hallway. The bald man was in that room, as well as another man with glasses.

"Okay Rachel, this will be easy. Have you ever had an MRI before?"

"Yes, I had one a few years ago when I got hurt playing soccer, but I had a concussion so I really don't remember much about it."

"Okay, this will be easy then. It will take about thirty minutes to get the whole thing done. You have to lay completely still so we can get a clear image of your brain."

I don't know if you've ever seen an MRI machine before, but it looks like a spaceship that's loud as hell and a claustrophobic's worst nightmare. Picture a narrow, plastic tube that you lay in.... yup, about accurate. They laid me down on a table outside of the machine, with my legs facing outwards. Then they put a foam wedge under my legs. "Here, how does that feel? You're going to be in there for a little while so we want you to be comfortable."

They gave me headphones and asked what my favorite type of music was so they could do their best to block out the loud noises that the machine gave off. "We'll put on music for you, but this is also a speaker so we can communicate with you. There is too much radiation for us to stay in the room." They then handed me a squeeze ball that was on a wire. "Take this too because if there is any reason that you need to stop, just squeeze the ball and we'll stop the machine and come back into the room for you." Damn. I wasn't mentally prepared for this...what the hell is about to happen right now?

"Okay Rachel, we're going to start now, are you ready?"

"Yeah I guess so," I exclaimed.

"Okay, we're going to get started."

They strapped my head down while I was laying there so it would be completely still, and then put a little claustrophobic cage over my head (as if the machine wasn't bad enough). They then pushed a button that backed me into the machine. Soon after, I heard the door shut, meaning that they had left the room. "Oh my God. Shit. This is actually scary AF. I didn't prepare myself for this at all," I thought. The machine then started making screeching, piercing noises that cut through my headphones like butter.

"I'm really going to sit here for a half an hour without moving at all? I never realized that I was claustrophobic until the second that they put a cage on my head and I was backed into this thing," When I get nervous, my hands sweat so I could feel them starting to pool up as I was grasping the squeeze ball for dear life. My forehead was sweating now too. "Oooh- Is it hot in here?"

I was slowly freaking out more and more with every second that passed by and I was getting very anxious. "Get me the F out of this thing." I thought. Every thirty seconds or so, I would move my legs a bit because my anxiety was so intense and I just wanted to wiggle out of there. "Rachel, make sure you are staying perfectly still," I heard them say through my headphones.

By the time that they pulled me out of the machine which felt like a lifetime later, my body was literally shaking from my hands to my feet. This time, the man with the glasses was there, and a new female who I hadn't seen before. She grabbed onto my sweaty hand while I was laying there...Embarrassing!

"So we just called your doctor and asked if we could add contrast to your MRI. We are going to inject the contrast into your veins to get a better image of your brain, okay?"

"Sure, whatever you need to do," I said.

In my head though, I was like, "Ughhh, what the F. Please don't put me in that machine for another minute. I can't wait for this shit to be over."

He stuck the needle in my arm to inject the contrast and backed me into the machine again. This time, it would only be for about ten minutes or so. After they left the room, I thought to myself, "That's a little strange though. Why would they have to call my doctor and ask to get better images if everything looked normal?" The ten minutes went by pretty quickly and before I knew it, they were pulling me out of the machine already. "Alright Rachel, you're all done. How was that, not bad right?" I wanted to say hell no, it was freaking terrible but I just smiled politely and hit him with a, "Yeah, it wasn't that bad!!!"

He brought me back to the changing area where all of my belongings were. I changed back into my clothes and was told to sit in the waiting area to wait for a copy of the MRI disk to bring to my doctor. I vividly remember texting my mom, sister, and work BFF who knew that I was getting an MRI. "Wow, that was so miserable! I hope I never have to do that again in my life!" About ten minutes passed, and the bald man was back again in the waiting room. "Rachel, can you come with me for a minute?" He led me to the little closet looking room again and I sat down on the bench.

"So... I don't know how to tell you this but we found something on your MRI today," he exclaimed. "We're not totally sure what it is, but it looks to be an aneurysm on your brain."

I instantly felt tears rushing to my eyes.

"Wait...what? Are you serious?"

Those were the only words that could come out of my mouth. My Poppy died from a brain aneurysm. "Try to stay calm. We are associated with many doctors at a prestigious hospital here in New Jersey. We've already sent one of the neurosurgeons your MRI and they are expecting your arrival to their emergency room as soon as possible. We don't want you to drive yourself though so you will either need to call someone to pick you up or we will call an ambulance for you."

Just like that, in the matter of seconds, my world changed completely, forever. My dad lived about five minutes from the MRI center but my first thought was to call mom because my dad was in New York City that day for work. Ring. Ring. Ring. Ring.

"Hello?"

"Mom? Are you around right now? You need to pick me up from the radiology center and bring me to the hospital. They found something on the scan of my brain and they think it might be a brain aneurysm! Are you home? Can you come? They don't want me to drive myself." I was in complete shock and just had total word vomit.

"They found something? I'm coming with Mike right now, hold on."

She lived about a half an hour away from the radiology center that I was at so it was going to take some time for her to get to me. I then called my manager to let her know that I wouldn't be calling in to any more meetings at work that day. While I was on the phone, the bald headed man signaled for me to follow him. We went back into the waiting area and crossed through to another door where there was an office that I could sit down and wait in. I couldn't help but think about what the people in the waiting area thought of me as I passed through, completely disheveled and bawling my eyes out.

I was really trying not to cry so hard though because I didn't know what an aneurysm was and I was afraid that the pressure from crying too hard would rupture it or something. I was about to call my dad until I saw that my mom was calling me again.

"Ray? Are you okay? I'm still about twenty minutes away. Maybe you should call daddy to see if he could get to you any sooner."

"Okay, I think he's in the city today, but I was about to call him anyway. If he's closer, I will just text you to meet me at the hospital."

Ring. Ring. Ring.

"Hello?"

"Hi Dad, are you on your way home from the city yet? I'm at the radiology center by your house and they think that they found an aneurysm on my brain. I need a ride to go to the hospital right now."

"Are you serious?" he blurted. "Yes, I actually just got home. I can be there in five minutes."

Two minutes later, I got a call from my sister.

"Hey Rach, what's up? I'm on my lunch hour and just figured I would call to say hi because I know you're working from home today. How was your MRI?"

My sister just so happened to call, randomly, during all of this chaos. I told her what was happening but told her that she didn't have to meet us at the hospital or anything until we had more details about what the hell was going on. She insisted on meeting us there, though. I remember waiting in the radiology office until my dad frantically came storming through the door.

"Hi, I'm her father, Alan. What did you see on the scan?"

"I think what we saw was an aneurysm. We're not doctors though, so we don't know for sure. You'll have all your questions answered when you get to the hospital and speak to the neurosurgery team."

We rushed to his car, and started making our way to the hospital. I think we literally passed like three other hospitals on our way there but they sent me straight to that specific hospital because it was one of the best in the state. It was a scary feeling to know that the other hospitals weren't going to cut it, but I felt at ease knowing that I was driving somewhere that would give me the best care possible.

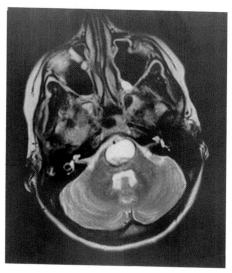

THE SCAN THAT CHANGED MY LIFE

CHAPTER 5

I remember the car ride to the hospital felt like a lifetime, but in reality, it was only forty minutes or so. We FINALLY arrived and followed signs in the parking lot to the emergency room entrance. As we pulled up to the doors, I saw my mom standing in the entryway waiting for me. I got out of the car and basically collapsed into her arms, crying again. Was this real life? What was happening? I tried so hard to prevent myself from looking things up on Google as we drove to the hospital because I knew everything that I read would definitely freak me out more. We went inside and checked in at the front desk. I was put on a stretcher almost immediately. My mom and I were left in the hallway because the emergency room was so busy at the time and no rooms were available.

My dad was parking his car and so was Mike. They ended up coming in at the same time. Within ten minutes after that, Rebecca showed up and so did Brandon. I thought that it was a very strange coincidence that everyone arrived at basically the same time. A short time later, one of the residents from the neurosurgery department came down to the emergency room to greet us.

"Hi, my name is Jenna. I'm one of the neurosurgery residents here. We've been expecting your arrival. We were sent your scans already and know what we're dealing with here." Everyone started to bombard her with questions but I was scared shitless, basically numb, and could barely get a word out. We were still in the hallway at that point.

Jenna drew a picture on her notepad so that we could visualize what an aneurysm looked like and what it did. I was immediately admitted and waited in the hallway until a room in the emergency room cleared out for me. Thank god because it looked like I had an army with me! They started an IV in my arm and we just waited in that room for a while. I was delivered a meal and then was eventually transferred upstairs to the neurology floor.

The surgeon that was assigned to my case was Dr. Graham. He came into my room to greet us all. It was Thursday and Dr. Graham explained that the following morning, he was planning to perform something called an angiogram on me. This was a procedure where he would go through my wrist or groin and basically thread a camera through my vein until it got up to my brain. He would then plug the aneurysm so that it wouldn't be a problem in the future. I was coincidentally at the end of my birth control pack at the time and was told to stop taking it right away because it could potentially cause blood clots or even worse, a stroke. Being that I have anxiety on a normal day, I was beyond the point of anxious panic.

The night of September 19 was a rough one, although my mom slept over at the hospital with me. She slept on one of those pull out chairs so that I wouldn't be alone. She's a trooper. That still didn't stop me from needing a Xanax to fall asleep though.

On Friday, September 20, 2019, I was scheduled to have my angiogram in the morning. I was a nervous wreck. Everyone told me that I wouldn't remember the procedure though, so that made me feel a little bit better. My nurses loaded me up with anxiety medication that morning to calm my anxious nerves.

When they were finally ready to wheel me down for my procedure, I was a bit groggy from the anxiety medication, but still alert enough to know what was going on. I'd finally got myself into a calm state and was ready to get this angiogram over with. Right before I was wheeled out of my room to head downstairs, my nurse stopped me, grabbed my hands, and started praying to me. That was it, that was all it took. I completely lost it again, sobbing.

Once I was wheeled into the operating room, I remember Dr. Graham had asked me to confirm my name, birthday, etc. "Okay now we're going to get started," he said.

I was waiting for someone to prick me and put me to sleep, but that never happened. I remember every second of the damn thing!!! I remember Dr. Graham trying to insert the camera through my wrist and was not successful, so he had to go through my groin instead. I guess I needed to be awake for this but just groggy- twilight, they call it? But I was under the impression that I would be asleep, not knowing anything about what was happening.

Dr. Graham would instruct me every ten seconds to hold my breath and then something weird would happen. One of the times that I held my breath, my ear felt like it was scorching hot. While still holding my breath, the hot sensation traveled from my ear, across my face, to my other ear. It felt like a fire was lit across my face. Another time that I held my breath, it's hard to put it into words but it looked like I saw strikes of lightning coming out of my eyes. It was the trippiest thing ever. And I remember it all happening. Yes, I was a little bit groggy but definitely not enough to forget what happened. Luckily, I don't remember it hurting or anything, although I got a huge bruise on my wrist from the unsuccessful attempt at weaving the camera up my arm.

I'm not sure how long the angiogram took all together, but it felt like so long before I was rolled into the recovery area to see my family. "Wow, that was it? I'm done with all of this forever now?" I said with excitement. What I was told next made me realize that my journey was far from over.

CHAPTER 6

"What you have is not an aneurysm, Rachel. From what I can see, it looks like you have something called a cavernous malformation. It's on your brain stem, but you are kind of in the gray area and we don't know what it is for sure unless we surgically enter your brain," Dr. Graham told me. "This case has turned into something that's now out of my realm, so I'm handing your case off to our Chief of Neurosurgery, Dr. Brady. Since it's Friday evening, he won't be back in the hospital until Monday morning. We will plan a family meeting for the early afternoon on Monday with him."

I couldn't completely process what I had just heard. "A cavernous huh? WTF is that?" I thought. The next two weekend days were probably the longest two days of my entire life. We researched Dr. Brady quite a bit that weekend. His resume was extremely impressive- he had so many awards, amazing reviews and publishings over the years. He was even part of the team of doctors that helped create the Chronic Traumatic Encephalopathy (CTE) rule for the NFL. I don't know if my memory just wants me to forget it, but I really don't remember too many details about that weekend clearly. I just remember watching TV from my hospital bed. Watching a TV show would pull me away from my reality. Whenever a commercial break came on though, reality would smack me in the face and my fears came flooding back as I realized what was actually happening to me. "Oh yeah. My life actually sucks right now." I also remember a coincidence which I believe was the first of multiple messages that I was receiving from heaven.

My dad and Mike were each reading the weekend newspaper and randomly found a one page article about Dr. Brady. This was before we ever even met the guy. What were the odds of that? It was extremely random. I remember watching the New York Giants game that Sunday, too. It was Daniel Jones's first ever start with the Giants and his first ever win with the Giants. I watched it in the common area of the hospital with my family because I didn't want to scream too loud at the TV in my room and disturb my roommate.

Brandon and I had tickets to go to the Giants game the following weekend. It was going to be Daniel Jones's first home opener of his career. "Don't worry Rach, you'll be there with me next week, I know it," Brandon kept saying to me. He was totally convinced that I'd be okay and would be able to go home on Monday night after we spoke with Dr. Brady. There was no doubt in his mind. He was so confident about it that he was starting to make me believe that it was true. Everyone was researching cavernous malformations online all weekend but there wasn't a ton of information or really a clear answer that told us if I would need to get this thing removed or not.

It was finally Monday, September 23, 2019. I think this day takes the cake for the worst day of my entire life. 11:30 AM rolled around before we knew it. My mom, dad, Mike, Rebecca and

Brandon were in my room with me. Dr. Graham was there as well as Dr. Brady. They wheeled in a portable monitor and pulled up my scan. Dr. Brady introduced himself to my family and just by his first sentence to us, I could tell that I was going to be in amazing hands with him. I was nervous to meet him because when hearing his title, I was expecting to meet a snooty surgeon- a surgeon who was good at what he did, but had no bedside manner. All business. But I was completely wrong. Something about Dr. Brady just exuded confidence. He made us all feel comfortable and safe by his presence and his first few words to us. He was very compassionate. I already felt a little calmer knowing that I was in care.

"Let's look at your MRI so we can show you what we see. Do you see that mass right here?" He pointed to the screen. "This is what is called a cavernoma, cavernous malformation, cavernous angioma, cav mal. It's located on the pons which is a part of your brain stem. It's about 3 cm. To be completely honest with you, I was expecting to come into your room today to see you on a ventilator in a coma. The fact that you are sitting up right now just talking to us is a miracle. Someone is definitely looking out for you up there because typically with a scan like this, I wouldn't expect a patient to look how you look right now."

I couldn't believe what he just said to me. I was having a few minor symptoms, but nothing to that extent. "A coma?!?!" I thought. I was just at the gym on Tuesday!!!!

"So where do we go from here? We like to use the analogy of a cavernoma as a raspberry on your brain. A cavernoma is basically a vascular tumor or cluster of abnormal blood vessels that leak blood on your brain and can cause you to have neurological symptoms. The cavernoma must have recently bled, which was causing you to have these strange symptoms. We believe that you were born with this too and it has just been growing and growing over the years. People live with cavernomas all of the time on the brain and never show any symptoms, but your situation is a bit trickier because it is located on your brain stem and it has already bled. The pons controls many things like regulating sleep, respiration, swallowing, bladder control, hearing, balance, taste, eye movement, facial expressions, facial sensation, and posture. I like to look at the brain stem like a fine piece of china, it's expensive real estate," Dr. Brady said. "The brain stem is extremely delicate, so you have an important decision to make. You can either wait it out and see what happens or we can choose to operate to remove the cavernoma. Waiting it out gives it the potential to bleed again and cause further symptoms, but having this surgery could cause temporary deficits that would all be reversible with rehab."

Either way, he assured me and kept assuring me that I would one day become a grandmother and live a long and healthy life.

The risk with waiting to see how things played out was that he could tell that I already had a few bleeds. Once you have one brain bleed from a cavernoma, you're more likely to have more. The problem was that a new bleed could be a small one where I could acquire minor symptoms that went away quickly, or I could have a major bleed that could kill me. It was like Russian roulette on your brain. What would you do?

I knew myself though. I knew that I wouldn't be able to live my life every day knowing that there was something in my brain that could rupture at any given point and kill me. I knew that I couldn't travel for my job if it had the potential to bleed when I was far away from my home. I needed to have it out. And I knew that right away.

After Dr. Graham and Dr. Brady left the room, we had a family meeting to discuss the pros and cons of having surgery versus not having surgery. My mom, dad, Rebecca, Mike, and Brandon were all there, taking turns discussing the pros and cons. Even though the final decision would be from me, each one of them had a big part in my decision.

CHAPTER 7

My surgery was scheduled for Thursday, September 26, 2019 but at the time, it was only Monday. They gave me the option to go home for a couple of days. I chose to stay in the hospital though because I knew that if I would've gone home, it would have been a lot harder for me to return back to the hospital.

I had some more things happen to me during the days leading up to my surgery that led me to believe that they were signs from my Grandma Selma in heaven. I had a dream that I was living in my old house in Manalapan and looked out of the window. Parked in the street was my grandma and grandpa's car. I didn't see them, but I saw their car there. When I was younger, they used to always come visit my sister and I on the weekends after we got out of dance class. Their car was always parked in that exact spot on the street. They would bring us our favorites which were chocolate Entemann's donuts and Vlastic pickles. (Sounds like a pregnant woman's dream, but no, just my strange sister and I as children- we loved that shit). I felt like that dream was a sign from my grandma and my grandpa letting me know that they were aware of what was going on and they were watching. It made me feel comforted.

I also got another sign from my grandma that week. I opened up Facebook and found a "memory" that I had posted on that day a few years earlier. It was a picture of my grandma with her three sisters. Some probably think it was just a stupid coincidence but I believe it was another sign from her. My grandma was a very strong, yet stubborn woman. I knew that she was doing everything she could to protect me from up there in heaven.

My first hospital roommate was a woman named Maria- she was a piece of work, I'll tell ya. Probably in her fifties or so. She just had surgery because of a stroke. There was a curtain between us, but she would talk to me and my mom from the other side of the curtain all day long. My mom helped her order her meals sometimes. My mom even went down to the gift shop to buy her sour candy one day because she asked for it. She was so hilarious. The day that we had a family meeting in my room where we discussed if I was going to have surgery or not, Maria was on the other side of the curtain, listening I assume. After making a decision about what I was going to do, my dad asked if anyone wanted some shoe leather (I don't know why my family calls it that, but it's basically an apricot fruit roll up). All of a sudden, from the other side of the curtain, we heard Maria say, "What's shoe leather? Can I have one?"

The Tuesday before surgery, Brandon slept over with me in the hospital so that my mom could go home for the night. In the middle of the night, I woke up in a panic. Brandon usually slept like a rock and wouldn't wake up through an avalanche, so I walked over to the nurses station, crying. My nurse pulled out a chair for me to sit there and hang out with her at 3 AM and ordered me a Xanax. I sat out there for a while until I finally calmed down enough to get some rest. Let me just say that prior to all of this happening, I never had a Xanax in my entire life. I really hate medicine like I've previously stated but I honestly don't know how I would have gotten through those days without taking Xanax. I popped those bad boys like candy.

The day before my surgery, Dr. Brady put in an order to move me into a private room a few doors down from my current room so that I wouldn't have any roommates. Partly because my mom slept over on a chair every night, and partly probably because I was a crazy psycho with anxiety leading up to my surgery and he wanted to give me some privacy as I panicked.

To be honest, I don't remember much else of the day before surgery. I just remember my sister coming to give me a pedicure and I remember taking a shower that night. "Wow, this could seriously be the last time I am standing up in a shower for a long time," I thought to myself.

I barely remember the morning of the surgery though. It's all just a blur to me. The only thing I do remember is the song that was playing in the operating room as I was rolled in... Señorita by Camila Cabello and Shawn Mendez.

"Do you like this song?" a resident asked me. "Yeah...not anymore."

My memory starts to get clearer post surgery when I was in the recovery area. My sister told me that surgery took about six hours. Only my mom and dad were allowed to come see me while I was just waking up. My mom was so overwhelmed with emotion that she almost passed out while walking into the recovery area.

I remember that I was lying flat and randomly looked up at the ceiling tiles. I couldn't see very well so I just kept my eyes shut for the most part because I was really dizzy. I remember hearing a man's voice that was taking care of me while I was still in the recovery area until an ICU bed opened up for me.

I couldn't really see the man that was taking care of me, but I pictured him as a short, stocky, bald man with glasses. I don't know why, that's just how I pictured him in my head. To this day, I still have no idea what he looked like.

I remember hearing my mom and dad's voice for the first time telling me that they were with me and that everything went well with my surgery.

"You did it, baby! You're all done now! You're amazing."

"Mom, dad! I can swallow my saliva now! I'm able to swallow again," I remember saying.

My parents told me that the nurse told them that I would likely need little to no therapy because I was able to move my hands and my toes right away. I don't know how much time passed, but I was eventually rolled up to the intensive care unit. At that point, I had to put a sleep mask over my eyes because I was so dizzy whenever I tried opening them. I remember my family telling me how nice the Neurology ICU was since I couldn't see it for myself. They said that it resembled a spaceship because it was so high tech and modern.

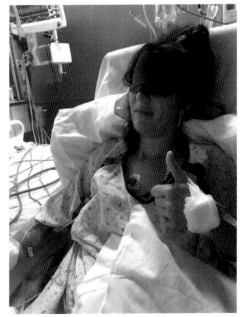

CHAPTER 8

My ICU bed faced the glass door that had a large number six written on it. The reason why I remember that so clearly was because that door as well as the whole room was spinning around like a windmill every time I removed my eye mask and tried to look at anything.

When anyone looked into my actual eyeballs, they said that my pupils were literally spinning around in circles. The first thing that I ordered from the hospital menu after my surgery was grilled cheese. Mike cut the sandwich up for me into tiny little squares and my mom sat by my bedside feeding me because I couldn't see shit to feed myself. I don't remember ever feeling anxious about not being able to open my eyes though. The only time that I felt afraid was when I felt sick to my stomach from the dizziness and was on the verge of puking. It didn't really help me remain calm that I couldn't see either.

I don't know why, but one of my biggest fears at the time was throwing up. Whenever I felt like I needed to, I would become terrified and work myself up into a frenzy. For God's sake I just had my skull cut open and I was more afraid of puking! I held a bucket in my lap, leaning over and getting ready to hurl.

My dad's girlfriend Heidi was in the room at the time and I remember so clearly hearing her voice speak to me. She could see that I was worked up and tried to calm me down. Her voice to me was so soothing. She was talking to me and counting out loud to get me to slow my breathing down and focus on other things. The feeling soon passed, and I was able to get through it without puking. Thank god.

Two or three days passed in the ICU. My eyes were still spinning in circles like a windmill. I literally had to keep my eyes closed every second of the day until I went to sleep for the night. Imagine how long those days felt? I heard so many voices of doctors and nurses coming in and out of my room throughout the day but I couldn't see. They would do neurological tests on me- remove my eye mask for a second to shine a light into my eyes to see if my pupils dilated, then put the mask right back on. By day four post surgery, the feeling of the windmill started to subside. Thank the good Lord. Four days felt like a long ass time, but I was just grateful that the feeling even went away at all- I could not imagine living a life where the room spun all the time. I would not be able to function.

Despite the spinning feeling going away, I was still feeling extremely dizzy, like my bed was a boat that was on choppy ass water. I also realized that I couldn't hear out of my left ear. In addition to that, I felt even weaker in my right hand. My right leg felt weak now too. I obviously hadn't tried walking or anything yet- I didn't know what I was capable of doing at that time.

We were told that my surgery was a success. The temporary deficits that I had acquired were reversible with therapy. The only thing that might not be able to be reversed was my hearing.

The hearing nerve on my left side had to be cut during surgery to access the cavernoma in my brain stem.

Because I was in the ICU, I had an ICU doctor as well. He would make rounds around the ICU floor each morning with the residents, stopping by each room. I don't recall this because I don't think the doctor ever said anything to me directly, but he said something to my family that was pretty alarming. He said something along the lines of "my post-operative scan still showed something on my brain stem." After further clarification, it was explained that my scan still showed "something" but all of the doctors believed that it was just post-operative blood that would reabsorb over time.

After about a week in the intensive care unit, I was transferred back up to the neurology floor again. For some reason, I just liked it better up there. I don't know if it was the fact that I was in the ICU that freaked me out or what, but I felt at ease being out of there.

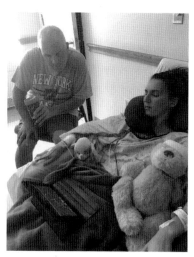

WATCHING THE GIANTS GAME BACK ON THE NEUROLOGY FLOOR WITH MY DAD

I didn't have a roommate when I first got upstairs and I thought that I would be lucky for the remainder of my time there. Most of the roommates that I had so far were a lot older than me; some confused and some setting off their bed alarms at 3:00 AM because they were trying to escape the hospital. At about midnight on the night that I was transferred upstairs, I heard the cleaning staff enter my room and start cleaning the bed beside me on the other side of the curtain. They just flipped on the lights like they had no regard that someone was on the other side of the curtain sleeping. "Damn it- this means another roommate," I thought. I listened closely to hear my new roommate's voice. To my surprise, she sounded pretty young.

The next morning, I wanted to introduce myself to her, so I opened up the curtain that was between us. Her name was Lauren. All I really knew was that she had just come upstairs the night prior from a procedure. She was such a nice girl and I was so happy to have someone young be my roommate. I was so used to women three times my age. I had an occupational and physical therapist come to see me everyday for about twenty minutes or so for the days that I was in the hospital. The occupational therapist gave me some therapy putty that I was instructed to use in my right hand whenever I had time throughout the day. Just squeeze it and work on strengthening the tiny muscles in my hand. I remember my hand was so weak that I wasn't able to hold onto my fork anymore when I ate.

The physical therapist's job was to get me up and moving. I was in a hospital bed all day so it was her job to get me walking post-surgery. The first time that we walked, I held on to a walker while she held onto my waist for support. There was a man following behind us with a wheelchair just in case I got tired and needed to sit down. I was able to make one full lap around the nurses station before I grew totally exhausted. I barely made it back to my room. When my family watched me loop around the hallway for the first time, they cried tears of happiness to see me walking.

I was wearing yellow hospital socks that were grippy at the bottom as I walked. I looked down at the bottom of my feet after my first walk. My left sock looked fine but my right sock looked like I just mopped the floor with it. I didn't realize it, but my right foot was so weak that it was dragging on the floor as I took each step.

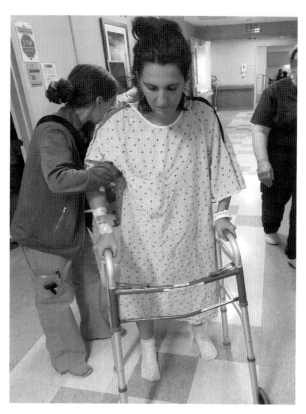

The next day, the physical therapist came back to get me walking again. This time, we walked about twenty yards before I started to see white dots and felt like I was going to pass out. I turned pale as a ghost. They immediately sat me down in the wheelchair that was behind me and rolled me quickly back to my bed. I was instructed to lay flat on my bed so that they could take my blood pressure which had dropped extremely low. White specks appeared in my line of vision until I could eventually only see white. I felt my heart pounding like it was about to fall out of my chest and my forehead started to sweat. I thought that at any second, I was going to pass out.

CHAPTER 9

On October 2nd, 2019, I was transferred to another hospital thirty minutes away to begin my inpatient rehabilitation program. The hospital did not let me drive in the car with my parents for the transfer; I had to be transferred over there by ambulance. I was so dizzy and so afraid that I would get carsick on a stretcher that was backwards on the ambulance. I was set up with a bucket in my lap just in case I had to puke as well as a styrofoam cup with ice chips that I could chew on. Let me just tell you, those ice chips were a gift sent from heaven. They saved me that day. The car ride was only thirty minutes, and the ice chips saved me about four times from projectile vomiting on the back of the ambulance window.

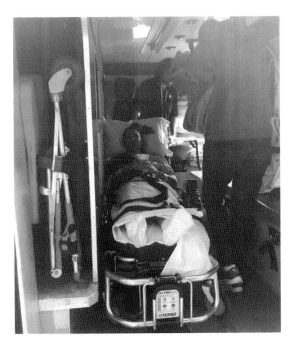

I got to the new hospital in the evening around dinner time. The nursing staff had a clean bed upstairs for me in their "neurology unit" for the night but said that I would be moved downstairs to their basic rehab unit in the morning when a room was ready. They said that I didn't qualify to stay in their "neurology unit". I didn't understand why until I was wheeled through the hallway though. This unit was for the severely impaired. The man across the hallway from my room was in an actual cage. "Ummm, does this door lock?" I asked my nurse. She chuckled, but I actually wasn't joking, I was scared. Thank God my family was still there with me. They helped me order my dinner but unfortunately had to leave shortly afterwards because there was a curfew for all visitors at 9:00 PM. My mom tried taking my cell phone with her that night so that I could get a first good night of sleep.

"Ummm, no. You are joking right? You are not taking that. Someone next door to me is in a cage. I need my phone on my nightstand just in case of an emergency," I said as I reached my hand out for her to place my phone in it.

I was terrified. This would be the first night without my mom sleeping over since I first came to the hospital, except for that one night that Brandon stayed with me. The nurse gave me Valium to try to get me to sleep but I literally tossed and turned the whole night. I just laid there for hours with my eyes shut, not able to sleep. The next morning, I met all of my new therapists. Everyday, I would have an hour each of all three therapies: speech, physical, and occupational. All of my therapists seemed very nice and I was eager to start the rehabilitation process and get better.

Physical therapy would help me strengthen my leg and get me walking with a better form, speech therapy would focus on rehabilitating my cognition, articulation and voice, and occupational therapy would work on strengthening my hand and arm, but also teach me how to shower, dress, and do daily activities again safely. I liked occupational therapy the best because what they did was really interesting to me. I don't know why I was so obnoxious during speech therapy, though. I found it hysterical. Maybe it was all of the "ooooh, ahhhhh, eeeee's" they had me doing or maybe I just felt awkward moving my face in weird ways while having my therapist and her student watch me like a hawk. Either way, that was definitely not my favorite thing.

Eventually, that day, they moved my room downstairs. This is where I thought I had another weird sign from heaven. My two lucky numbers are 15 and 21 and I was rolled into room 1520-001. What are the chances? Those are the most random numbers ever. Again, I was rolled into a room where there was a vacant bed next to mine. "Sweet! No roommate." I thought. When looking at who was getting therapy around me in the gym, I felt like I didn't belong there. I felt like I was in a nursing home to be honest. I was by far the youngest patient there. Just a few months earlier, I was on a work trip in Hawaii alone. Now, I couldn't even go to the bathroom without notifying my nurse that I wanted to get out of my bed.

The second night for me was a little better than the first night. I was starting to get a bit more acclimated to my new environment. I just kept saying to myself, "You are here with a purpose. Do what you gotta do to get the hell out sooner, and get better quicker." That evening's thought was broken up by a man who came into my room, pulling a stretcher with someone on it. "Damn it. A new roommate?!"

As he pulled the stretcher in my room, I quickly realized that it was Lauren! The girl who was my roommate from the other hospital! What were the chances of that? I was so excited!! As much as it sucked being in rehab, Lauren there truly made it a little better. Over the next week there, and countless conversations with each other, we really bonded and looked out for one another. It was so nice to have someone closer to my age as a roommate that I could relate to. I found out that she had something located on her brain stem like me, but it wasn't a cavernoma. All I knew was that she had the mass biopsied, rather than surgically removed like I did. Because our situations were a little different, it left us with different deficits.

One of her legs was completely numb which I didn't have, but I required speech therapy, which she didn't need. It was fascinating to me that although we both had recent trauma to the same part of our brain, it affected us so differently. I was on so much medication at the time, but no painkillers from the time that I was in the ICU until that day. From the second I got out of my surgery, I refused them and stuck to Tylenol only because I'm so anti-medicine.

After about two weeks with my stitches in, they were ready to be removed. I had to take Xanax before the rehab doctor took them out because the incision site was on my head behind my left ear. I never had stitches before, let alone stitches on my head. I remember laying down on my stomach, just staring at my pillow. The doctor pulled on the stitches one by one and unlaced them slowly from my head. It wasn't a fun feeling to remember but at least I stayed calm. To pass time in the late afternoon each day after having therapy, my family would hang out with me in the common room, take me outside for some fresh air, or order some takeout. I would look forward to the visiting hours. It felt normal to see them!

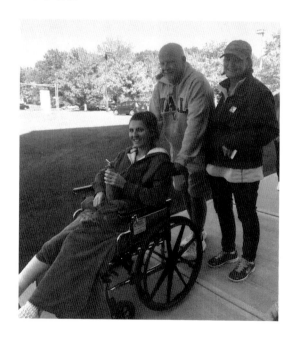

I was on multiple medications post-surgery and some of them had to be taken at the same time every day- a shot in my belly (a blood thinner) and an oral steroid that reduced the swelling in my brain. I had a journal where I wrote down the exact medication I was taking at the exact time that it was administered to me each day because I was having so many issues with the nursing staff there.

For instance, my nurse would tell me all of the pills that she was giving to me and then a half an hour later, after I had taken everything, I would find a random pill on my nightstand that she had left behind. I thought that I was given everything that I needed to take, and then I would get confused because I didn't know which pill was left there. Another time, my nurse gave me my evening medicine, listing out loud what she was giving me as I wrote it down in my journal. After taking all of the medication, I then found out that she also gave me some kind of muscle relaxer without my knowledge. WTF- It felt like abuse or something! The nurses were all over the place and it was a total shitshow. I couldn't imagine if my cognition was not intact and I wasn't able to advocate for myself and my care.

There were times that I would hit my call bell to ask for Tylenol after counting the minutes until I was finally allowed to take another dose because I was in so much pain. It would sometimes take the nurse over an hour to bring it in, though. There was also an instance where I was given my steroid and then twenty minutes later, my nurse came back into my room to give me the same dose of the steroid again. I don't know if the nurses were just assigned too many patients at a time, but if I didn't track every pill that went into my mouth, I would have definitely been given something twice at some point.

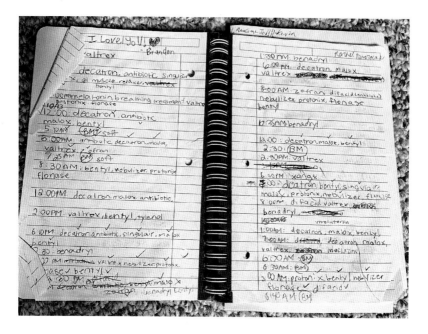

I couldn't help but think about all of the older patients at the facility who couldn't advocate for themselves- it was really, really sad. It was honestly borderline abusive, especially after going through something so traumatic. I had to be tapered off of my steroids slowly until I stopped them completely. The steroids were brutal on my body- they gave me acne on my shoulders, neck, and face, and they gave me something called "moon face". If you don't know what that is, it's exactly what it sounds like- My face blew up like a balloon.

They also made me want to eat everything in sight. I would literally wake up in the middle of the night starving and have a PB and J sandwich on my nightstand ready to inhale at 2:00 AM because I would wake up ravenous. Every day, I would take less and less of the steroid, and everyday, my headaches grew worse and worse. I remember one night as I was taking a lower dose,

Brandon and his sister were visiting me. I was in sooooo much pain that night.

I felt the swelling from my brain going into my neck, lymph nodes and running through my temples. It honestly felt like the swelling was fluid in my temples that was dripping down into my neck. I had two ice packs glued to each of my temples to try and numb the pain from my head. It was so painful, I wanted to cry, but the pressure from crying would just make it hurt more. I felt bad that Brandon's sister had to see me in so much pain like that because she wasn't there to see me everyday and I didn't want her to have that bad mental image of me. I just couldn't hide the agony that night. It was freaking brutal. Brandon eventually called a nurse into my room. "She's saying that she feels the swelling in her lymph nodes, and it's hard for her to swallow. Is that normal?" The nurse examined me, but said it was okay, and it was normal to experience some pain when tapering off of the steroids. SOME pain?! This was a little more than some pain girlfriend.

CHAPTER 10

That night, the pain was so unbearable that I didn't sleep. The next day, after barely making it through therapy, my family came, as usual, during visiting hours. My parents asked my nurse to request the on-call neurologist who was in the hospital to come examine me because the pain just wasn't letting up. It took a few hours for her to finally show up. The "neurologist" was actually a resident and she seemed very agitated that she had to go out of her way to see me. "Is this a true emergency because I'm in the middle of completing rounds right now?" She said, with a major attitude, as if having to stop by my room was a nuisance. She told us that the pain that I had was likely because the steroid's job was to suppress the swelling and now that I was tapering off of them, I felt the pain. I was basically told to just suck it up and deal with it until the pain dissipated.

An hour or so after the rude resident left, my family started to notice that my face started to droop very slightly on my left side. They called my nurse in before her shift ended and before a new night nurse would be starting her shift. My nurse again confirmed that I was okay and it was all due to the steroid taper.

My anxiety started to ramp back up again. My dad realized that I was internally freaking out so he started to wheel me in my wheelchair into the common room to take my mind off of the pain and new strange symptoms.

As he started pushing me down the hallway, my two new night nurses came running up from behind us. "We just read the shift notes from your day nurse- we see a visible droop. Why are you taking her to the common room??!!! Bring her back to her room immediately!!! Please REMAIN CALM, Rachel! It's going to be OKAY." They hovered over me, yelling and freaked me out because they were both freaking the F out, no exaggeration.

As soon as I got back onto my bed from the wheelchair, one of the nurses started doing a neurological check on me. "Wiggle your toes, push your foot like you're hitting the gas pedal into my hand, squeeze my fingers, raise your arms up and close your eyes. It's okay sweetie, don't cry. You're able to do it all- those are all good signs," she said to me as I was hysterical.

She then turned to my family and said that she was going to call an on-call neurosurgeon to come examine me. After another long hour of waiting, he came down to my room from the main hospital and did the same neurological exam on me. He also ordered a CT scan to make sure that everything looked stable internally on my brain. My family stayed as late as they were allowed to, until visiting hours were over- 9:00 PM. We all just assumed that the CT scan would be done in the morning, so I went to sleep for the night.

THE SLIGHT FACIAL DROOP THAT
I DEVELOPED IN REHAB

At midnight, I was woken up by my nurse. "Wake up honey, it's your turn to go upstairs for your CT scan", she stated. She transferred me from my bed to a stretcher, and wheeled me upstairs to the hospital's emergency department. The scan took literally five minutes and before I knew it, I was back downstairs in bed. I stayed up for a while, waiting to get my results. It was so late at that point so after a while, I finally just fell back asleep. I was woken up at 6:00 AM again by the same nurse.

"They want to repeat your CT again to see if there are any changes from your midnight scan," she said. "I'm going to bring you upstairs for the scan now." Again, I was transferred to a stretcher and brought upstairs. This time, when she took me back downstairs to my room, I didn't fall back asleep because it was already the morning. An hour or two later, I got a call on my cell phone from my mom. "Rach, they just called me with your CT results- they see some blood on your scan that doesn't look normal. It didn't change from last night to this morning but we're on our way there now. Daddy is coming now to pick up the CT disk, and drive it to Dr. Brady so he can read the results to compare it to your last scan with him." Immediately I found myself crying again. This can't be happening. I hung up with my mom and started sobbing into my hands. The cries hurt my head. There was a curtain separating Lauren and I, and she opened it as soon as she heard me.

"What's going on? Are you okay?" she asked.

"They found blood on my scan and I don't know what it's from. I had a nightmare a couple of nights ago that I needed a second brain surgery and that is my biggest fear. I can't do it again."

I know I might have jumped the gun on that one and expected the worst, but I honestly just wanted to prepare myself for the worst. I'm always like that. Mike and my mom showed up after what felt like a long ass time. At the same time, my dad arrived to pick up the disc to drive it to Dr. Brady. Don't ask me why it couldn't have just been emailed or scanned over, it had to do with the quality of the scan being better on a physical disc.

Once my dad arrived back with me and an hour or so passed, Dr. Brady called my mom's cell phone. She put it on speaker for us to hear.

> "We just looked at your scan from midnight last night and 6:00 AM this morning. The doctors over there were worried that they saw some blood on your scan. I just compared it to your post-operative scan here and it looks like what they see is

just residual bleeding that is the same from your last post-operative scan here. Don't worry, that is nothing new. Since you do still have residual bleeding from surgery though, I am going to take you off of the blood thinners that you're on. We believe that the reason for the droop on your face is because you were tapered off of the steroids too quickly. We are going to put you back on them, and do a slower, longer taper. We also got the results back from your biopsy after surgery and it is confirmed that it was a cavernoma that was removed. I am so happy that you made the choice to have this thing removed because it was like a ticking time bomb in your brain."

Wow. That was a crazy relief to hear. I felt like I could finally sigh and release the stress that was building up within me. Because he wanted to put me back on steroids, it would mean that my immunity would be lower, therefore the incision on my head would have a harder time healing. Also, my droop was looking a little bit worse than when it first happened and now my left eye wouldn't close all the way.

A day or two later, the doctor that removed my stitches came by to check the healing scar. He noticed that my healing skin where my stitches once were looked a little "funky". No one at my rehab wanted to be responsible for a possible infection, so no one wanted to touch me. They suggested sending me back to Dr. Brady for an office visit so he could take a look for himself.

The only way that I was able to get there was via ambulance so again, I was loaded up in a stretcher, ice chips and all, into the ambulance to see Dr. Brady. Road trip!!! I remember when we first got there, we saw Dr. Brady and his Physician's Assistant (PA), Eliza, enter into the elevator. I felt an automatic sense of relief when I saw the two of them. My experience at rehab so far had been hell and I felt safe again being close by to the two of them. Tears came to my eyes as I said hello and reached my hand out for Dr. Brady's. He grabbed my hand back and said, "Don't cry! We'll be with you soon. It's so great to see you."

CHAPTER 11

After waiting in the waiting room, we were called back to see Dr. Brady. He took a good look at my incision. "I am happy with the way that this is healing. The reason why it hasn't closed fully yet is because the steroids have been preventing it from closing, but by no means is it 'infected.'" Phew. More good news! It just so happened that the day that I went back to the hospital to see Dr. Brady, Lauren was also at the hospital for the day to meet with her surgeon to go over her biopsy results. As I was getting loaded back into my ambulance for the trip back to rehab, I saw Lauren down the street getting pushed in a wheelchair by her boyfriend. Lauren was crying and he mouthed to us that it wasn't a good time as we were waving to get her attention.

"Oh no," I said as I was lifted and strapped into the rear of my ambulance. Lauren doesn't know this, but as we were driving away in the ambulance I cried. And cried. And cried so hard for her. I didn't know what news she got, but she didn't seem happy about it. And I was so upset for her. I didn't even know the news but I knew that it wasn't great and that absolutely broke my heart. As we got onto the highway, I just remember every bump that we hit was so miserable. Not only was it nauseating but it was so incredibly painful in my head and my neck.

That night started the first of many long nights. My stomach would be okay all day, and then as soon as it hit one or two in the morning, I would wake up from my sleep feeling terribly sick. Extremely bad stomach aches and in and out of the bathroom all night. I thought I had a stomach bug or something. The strangest part about the whole thing was that this would only occur at night after I went to sleep, but never during the day. My mom was told by one of her friends who was a nurse to request having me tested for "c-diff". This was something commonly spread in hospitals that was super contagious. It caused inflammation of the colon. They drew my blood to test for it but it took some time for the results to come back. The next morning, my nurse came to speak with me. "The results came back that you tested positive for the DNA of c-diff. Because of the fact that it's highly contagious, your roommate is going to have to pack up her things and move to a different room. You will need to be in isolation."

Before Lauren was wheeled out, I exchanged phone numbers with her. Apparently it was contagious because when the germs left the body, they became "spores" that lived for long periods of time on the surfaces around me. When I looked up c-diff online, it didn't make any sense to me that I had that. You had to have 10-15 watery stools per day and I had zero...

The real way to test if you actually had c-diff was by a stool sample. The blood test that I was given just showed that my body carried the DNA for c-diff, which meant that I was exposed to it at some point. That didn't mean that I actively carried it, though. I think that they were just erring on the side of caution. I felt like I was an alien or something- not only did they stick a "hazardous" sign on the outside of my door, but I was not allowed to leave my room whatsoever, and all of my therapists had to come to my room to do therapy.

What was the point of that? Speech was okay to do from my room, but the whole point of being at a rehab facility was to take advantage of their gym to use the equipment for occupational and physical therapy sessions. If that wasn't bad enough, they hung gowns and gloves on the outside of my door, and even if a nurse came in for a second, they would have to "suit up". No one could come into the room unless they had a gown and gloves on.

The c-diff ordeal brought to light my new sensitivity to medication. It took three different medications before they finally found one that didn't make my lips and tongue swell up. The problem was, I could never swallow large pills and the only medication that didn't give me a reaction happened to be a huge horse pill. Their solution to that was mixing up a concoction of crushed up pill with banana or crushed up pill with chocolate pudding. Yep. It was as nasty as it sounded. "We don't feel totally convinced that you have c-diff but we want to be cautious about it," said an infectious disease doctor to me. This made my already horrible experience at rehab even worse. It didn't help that I had to track medicine to make sure I was receiving proper doses at proper times. "Don't leave me here. Please. Just take me home," I said to my mom that night.

I was so done. I wanted to go home. Visiting hours had just ended, but my mom disregarded that. She took a pillow and a blanket, and laid on the metal bed frame where Lauren's bed used to be. She wasn't going to leave me alone that night. I tried to tell her to come into the bed with me, but she refused.

My head pain felt so much better being back on steroids again. It suppressed the pressure that I was feeling from the swelling in my brain, but I was terrified for the final taper again although it would be slower this time. The bad thing was that the longer that I was on these steroids, the lower my immunity would be and the longer it would take the huge incision on my head to heal.

The day came before I knew it where I had "graduated" from my rehab program and was finally able to go home. Thank you Lord. Although that was the end of my journey at inpatient rehab, I still required several intensive therapy months at outpatient rehab. The droop on my face had improved, but my right leg was still very weak when I walked and it was hard to lift my leg with each step so it wouldn't drag on the floor. I had to use a one-arm crutch to walk without falling over.

I required vestibular therapy to work on the vision that made me so dizzy. My right hand was still really weak too. Besides that stuff, we decided that I didn't really need speech anymore, so I was planning to have my sister (a speech therapist) work with me a little from home and give me some things to do. I literally couldn't get out of there quicker. If I could run, I would have- I had just about had it with that hell hole. The past few weeks were easily the worst couple of weeks that I had in my entire life. I was so excited to go home.

CHAPTER 12

Arriving home on October 17, 2019 for the first time was so weird. We pulled up to my house and saw a big sign on my front door that said "WELCOME HOME RAY". I struggled to get out of the car and inside of the house where I discovered that my dad and sister had decorated for me. I couldn't help but notice that my work laptop was still in the same place that I had left it on September 19 while I went for my MRI on my lunch break.

There was so much that has happened since that day that nobody was ever expecting. Yes, what I went through was traumatic for me but I always think about everyone else in my family that had to go through that too. I couldn't imagine waiting in the operating room waiting area for hours while someone that I loved was having brain surgery. When you think about brain surgery, you think scary. You think serious.

It only takes one small error, and it could be fatal. I never really thought about that though while I was going through it. I thought about having a cavernoma in my brain and knowing how it would negatively affect my life if it stayed there. The second that they found something was the second that I knew it needed to be removed. How could I go on work trips, vacations, snowboarding, out to eat, virtually do anything and just "watch it" when I knew that it could bleed or explode in my brain stem at any time? It was just a no-brainer for me (no pun intended).

I remember feeling extremely relaxed and relieved to finally be home. "Wow it literally feels like I just took like five Xanax or something," I remember saying as I sunk back into my recliner chair, so happy not to hear hospital beeps, crying patients, nurses chit chatting. The quiet was total bliss. On my second night back at home, I took a new medication right before bedtime. I don't remember what it was for or what the name of the medication was, but at about 10:00 PM, I felt my lips swelling up and itching.

My mom and Brandon were there with me, trying to look into the back of my throat with their phone flashlights to see if it was narrowing or closing up. I couldn't really tell if it was myself because half of my face, lips and tongue were numb so it was hard for me to know what the feeling felt like. By 10:30 PM, they decided to take me to the emergency room near my house. Better be safe than sorry, right? My mom helped me hobble quickly into the front seat of my car, and Brandon drove us all there. It was nighttime, and only my second time being in the car, so I was really dizzy. I brought a vomit bag with me just in case, but we were under ten minutes away from the closest hospital, so I thought I would be okay as long as I shut my eyes the whole time.

Since it was a possible allergy to medication, the nurse in the emergency room brought me to a room right away and I saw the doctor almost immediately. After examining me, he believed that it was just a sensitivity to the new medication, ordered some "magic mouthwash" for me, and ordered a discharge after giving me some Benadryl. The "magic mouthwash" was a numbing agent that I could swish around in my mouth when it felt irritated. Since I only took the medication nightly for a short period of time, I was told to continue taking it but now with a dose of Benadryl too.

We decided that I would complete a week or two of home therapy before starting outpatient therapy because I was on the steroids and so susceptible to catching anything. We had a nurse come to the house, a physical therapist, and an occupational therapist. The nurse would take my blood pressure, temperature, ask me how I'm feeling, examine my healing incision, etc. My physical therapist was horrible. He gave me a sheet of paper and basically said "do this". When I worked with him, I would literally laugh in his face. I don't know if I laughed because I just felt awkward or if he just sucked but I legitimately couldn't control it. I felt so rude. I hoped that the inappropriate laughs would go away as my brain healed more. I think that the physical therapist's clientele was mostly elderly patients who had just broken their hip or something; not a 25 year old with a neurological condition.

My occupational therapist, however, was awesome. She was so innovative and would find any random item in my house to make into therapy somehow. It seemed like she would work great with any one, at any age, rehabbing anything. Her personality and positivity was very refreshing to me. The steroids made my appetite off the charts. I couldn't wait to eat my next snack before I finished the first one. I'm normally not like that at all though but I had been eating like an absolute freaking maniac. I can't even explain it to you.

Everyday that my steroid taper lowered, my head hurt more and more. It's hard for me to describe how that pain felt- it wasn't a normal type of headache. The pressure that was in my head was truly indescribable. I kept thinking to myself, "Okay- when I'm off of the steroids completely, it might suck for a few days but I'll just have to suck it up and get through a couple of bad days and then things will get better." Being off of steroids was obviously better for me in the long run too.

The day that I totally came off of the steroids wasn't a great one for me, as expected. My appetite changed from being hungry all of the time to no appetite at all. Even just the thought of food made me nauseous. I was on Tylenol around the clock because the pain that I had from the second that I woke up to the second that I laid down to sleep in the evening was excruciating and completely unbearable. The pain that I felt made me sick. The next couple of days, I wanted no part of that guy who was my physical therapist. To me, he was just a big annoying idiot. My mom would say to him, "Yeah, she's in a lot of pain right now, just bear with her" because while completing the exercises, I wouldn't say a word. I honestly just wanted him to get out of my face and get out of my house but I was too polite to say anything even remotely close to that.

My first "outing" was at the Starbucks by my house. My mom and Mike were taking me. The date was October 29, 2019. My home nurse came to the house earlier that morning, looked at my incision, and said it looked like it was healing very well. As we walked to the car that afternoon to go to the Starbucks though, my mom looked at my incision as I was in the sunlight and had a different opinion about how it looked (not in a good way). For some reason, I didn't want to see the wound on my head at all, ever, until it was a completely healed scar. From the day that I woke up from my surgery, I hadn't looked at it one time and didn't plan to.

Luckily, we had Dr. Brady's PA, Eliza's cell phone number and snapped a picture to text her. As we waited for her reply back, my mom and Mike still insisted on going to Starbucks to try and take my mind off of everything and enjoy my first time out.

The Starbucks was right around the corner from my house. I used to stop there on my way to work, before I went snowboarding with Brandon, before heading to the beach. Basically all of the normal stuff that I did. It was weird that I was now at that same coffee shop with my mom and Mike, in a totally different state. I thought that we were just going to go through the drive thru, but when we got there, they pulled into a spot and convinced me to go inside.

Not only was this my first time out of the house but now it was the first time that I was going out in public. I limped into the coffee shop with my crutch and immediately felt eyes drawn to me. "I wonder what happened to that girl," I knew people were thinking. I was so self-conscious there. I couldn't wait to leave the second that I walked through the door. We sat down with my slice of pumpkin bread and salted caramel hot chocolate. Right at that moment, Eliza texted my mom back. "She said that she wants us to come into the office at 2:30 today to have Dr. Brady look at the incision in person," my mom said.

Instantly, I felt my nerves which automatically made my stomach hurt. "Is that all she said? Should I be worried?" I asked. No more pumpkin bread for me. I couldn't even take a bite. We sat there for about twenty minutes, where I let them both pick apart my untouched pumpkin slice. I had home occupational therapy that day after our outing and now, before my appointment with Dr. Brady.

"I don't want to do any therapy today- can we please call and cancel?"

"No," my mom said, "I think it will be a good distraction for you."

After we made it home and got settled in, the occupational therapist knocked on my front door. I was really not in the mood for therapy though. "She wanted to cancel today because we have to go to her neurosurgeon soon because the incision on her head might be infected and she's anxious," my mom said to my therapist. Mom was good at getting straight to the point, that's for sure. My therapist still worked me pretty hard, showing no mercy. My mom was right- it was a great distraction. I wanted to work my hardest during therapy, but I had such bad pressure in my head and now my incision was throbbing and felt hot. I had a gut feeling that something just wasn't feeling right so I think that that's why my nerves were so bad.

On the drive to Dr. Brady's office which was connected to the main hospital, I felt so sick. It was a forty-ish minute drive, and I just sat there in the backseat chewing on ice and using a neck pillow to support my wobbly head. I learned that the neck pillow absorbed some of the shock created by going over bumps in the road- I was so sensitive and felt so fragile and weak. We finally made it there and were brought to the check up room.

When I saw Eliza and Dr. Brady, I could barely do anything but stay silent in pain so my mom did most of the talking for me. It hurt to do anything at that point and it was just getting worse. After the two of them looked at my incision, Dr. Brady said, "I'm not happy with the way that it's looking. I think that we should re-admit you through our emergency room to find out what kind of infection you have brewing here. I also want to call in the infectious disease team and the wound care team to examine you and get their opinions about how we should proceed." I'm not going to lie, my mother and I were kind of relieved to hear about my readmission to the hospital. We thought that:

A. It would be a lot better having nurses there to watch me around the clock when I was this fragile

B. The infection was probably the reason why I felt so horrible so by the time that we left the hospital after treating the infection, I thought that I would be feeling like a million bucks again.

Mike went to get the car to pick us up, and my mom helped me hobble my way out of the office into his car. It was a quick two minute ride to the emergency room entrance where we got dropped off. We had a pack of surgical masks with us and planned to keep one on during the whole ordeal because emergency rooms were always known to be germy and my immunity was still fragile.

CHAPTER 13

The emergency room was very full that day so there wasn't a room available for me. They put me on a stretcher in the hallway, but I didn't really mind because I thought that it would only be a short amount of time before I was admitted and sent back upstairs to the neurology floor. My dad had shown up at that point too. He couldn't sit anywhere but down the hallway from me because there was no room beside me- I was literally next to the bathroom entrance in the hallway. Finally, I saw two of the neurosurgery residents approaching. I recognized Jenna but I didn't know who the other resident was. He looked really young to me. "Hi Rachel, it's good to see you again!" Jenna said. "We just have to take a sample from your incision and bring it to the lab to see if it grows any bacteria overnight. That will tell us what kind of infection you have going on and how we are able to treat it."

Next, she had me turn my head to show her the incision. "Oooh. Yeah. I can see that your wound is a little opened at the top. Okay, are you ready? I'll try to do this as quickly as I can." She then grabbed a hold of my incision behind my left ear and started to squeeze it like she was trying to pop a stubborn pimple. Let me just say, an incision that was on my head and already on fire made it all the more incredibly painful. Mind you, I was still in the middle of the hallway for this part. Next, my emergency room nurse drew my blood to do some kind of testing to make sure that the infection didn't travel into my bloodstream. I've always been okay about getting my blood drawn, as long as I didn't have to look. It seemed like he literally drew a pint of blood out of my veins.

I noticed that my emotions were out of whack again when I called Brandon to let him know that I was in the emergency room again. He asked me why I was there, and I burst out into uncontrollable laughter. Laughing to the point where I couldn't even get words out and had to hand the phone over to my mom to explain to him what was going on. Nothing was even remotely funny, obviously, so I didn't know what the laughter was for.

The neurosurgery team also ordered a CT scan to make sure that the infection was just superficial and hadn't traveled into my brain. I had a bunch of MRI and CT scans done from my first stay at the hospital. Since realizing that I'm super claustrophobic, the only way that I was able to get through these tests was by taking a Xanax or Valium to calm down. Since I had been through so many of these scans, I figured that I would try doing this scan without medicating prior. Plus, CT scans are only like, a minute long. I could do that, right?

Uhhhh, wrong. I literally freaked TF out. The man who ran the machine set me up, then left the room due to the radiation that the machine gave off. As soon as he left the room, I had a really bad panic attack. I haven't had those often in life, but I think that was definitely considered one. I started hyperventilating and was screaming, "I don't want to be in here!!! Get me out PLEASE!!!" Of course, this was like the only time that no microphone was attached to me for him to hear me. Or maybe he DID hear me but was just ignoring me on purpose to see if I could last the one minute.

I remember he came back into the room after it was finished and I was shaking, hyperventilating, and crying. Fun times!!! He opened the double doors so that my mom and dad could come into the room to calm me down. They actually had to order me Xanax after I was rolled back to the hallway in the emergency room. So much for trying to not have that! Since my original appointment with Dr. Brady that day was at 2:30 PM and it was now 6:30 PM, I was starving. Luckily, I always kept snacks in my purse. I had pretzels with me to hold me over. As a patient, you weren't allowed to eat your own food in the emergency room, but I just kept popping a pretzel under my mask every few minutes after my nurse walked by.

Out of the blue, we saw Dr. Brady approaching us with like four or five residents trailing behind him. I kind of felt like a big deal- he was the big man on campus as the chief of neurosurgery and I couldn't imagine that he went down to the emergency room very often. "How are you guys doing? I can't believe that you are still down here. I am going to make a call to get you a room upstairs right away." I felt like he was always looking out for me. My guy! Dr. Brady had told me before my first surgery that he had a son who was my age and a daughter that was a bit younger than me. I couldn't help but think that he looked out for me as if I were one of his own. I was the "VIP" he would joke. He just had a way about him that made my family and I feel comforted and safe always.

As soon as he left us, my mom and I sent my dad to get us some food down the street from the hospital because we were absolutely starving and realized that I had missed the window to order myself dinner from the cafeteria. We assumed that I would be transferred up to my room by the time that my dad got back. A half an hour later, dad was back but we were still waiting downstairs in the emergency room. Apparently, my room was ready but it was now a shift change for the nurses upstairs, so I would have to wait a few more minutes. Twenty more minutes or so passed until they had someone come down to get my stretcher to wheel me upstairs.

When we arrived at my room, the cleaning staff was still in the middle of cleaning it, so the transport man locked my stretcher and left me in the hallway outside of my room. At that point, if I didn't eat something, I was going to lose it so I grabbed one of the take out containers from my dad, and started shoveling noodles down my throat in the middle of the hallway outside of my room. I didn't even care what it looked like. I'm sure that noodles were flying left and right but I was just ravenous. Ten minutes later, we were able to go into my room and settle in. No roommate again- yes! My dad helped us unpack what we needed, and then decided to head out because it was getting late. My mom stayed with me; she is my girl forever. We were basically attached at the hip LOL!

I wasn't THAT lucky though with the no roommate thing- a new one arrived in the middle of the night who was just admitted from the emergency room due to a stroke. Her name was Elizabeth. She was probably in her 50s. I was able to talk with her a bit the next morning. She was very sweet. Since they basically squeezed the life out of my incision the day before, I was in immense pain that morning. We had to wait to see if the sample that they took from my incision grew bacteria. If it grew bacteria, they would have to see which kind of bacteria it was to determine which antibiotics they would use to treat it.

Since I was supposed to be doing physical therapy and a ton of walking, I did a lap around the hospital floor with my walker before growing exhausted each afternoon. I had the window side of the room so every time that I walked past Elizabeth's bed, she would cheer me on. "You go girl! Bless you!" She was funny as hell too. We watched Impractical Jokers together on TV the second night that she was there and even though it would hurt my head to laugh, we were both cracking up together.

When lunch time rolled around on the third day, Mike and my mom went out for lunch to get some fresh air for a bit. The surrounding town outside of the hospital was nice- there were a lot of places walking distance away. The plan was that I'd take a nap while they were out. My room was right next to the nurses station, so it was really loud there though. I don't know why I remember this so vividly, but while I was trying to close my eyes that day, I was hands down in the worst pain that I had experienced since the start of this whole ordeal. Even worse than I felt right out of the craniotomy. I felt like I was going to pass out from the amount of pain that I was in.

The next day, we found out that some bacteria had grown in the lab from the sample that they took from my incision. It was a Staph infection. This type of bacteria normally comes from your own skin. My incision was right along my hairline behind my ear, so my hair always got caught in it. As soon as they found out what kind of infection I had, the infectious disease team came into my room to discuss some possible antibiotic options with me. Since I had grown such a sensitivity to medication after my surgery, almost everything made my tongue and lips swell.

They wanted to make sure that I was given something that my body could handle. Also, to make things more complicated, the antibiotic had to be small or crushable since I couldn't swallow large pills. They came to the decision to give me an antibiotic through an IV. I have taken this particular antibiotic orally before during my "c-diff" treatment and had a reaction to it, but they told me that the IV version was different. They also talked about the possibility of having my incision surgically cleaned out, but they wanted to speak with Dr. Brady about it first.

Dr. Brady shot that idea down right away. He truly believed that the infection was just superficial but also said that I had been through enough already so he didn't want to have me go through another procedure unnecessarily. We were just going to wait to see if the antibiotics worked their magic before moving to plan B. Because my medication was through an IV, I had to stay in the hospital for the full course of antibiotics which was four more days. My Halloween would be spent in the hospital this year, but I didn't mind. It's not like I was planning to do anything anyway. At first, I felt okay with the IV but after a couple of doses, I felt burning throughout my veins. Dr. Brady was really good at making sure that he stopped by at some point each day whenever he was in the hospital. I'd be lying if I didn't say it was the highlight of the day- best doctor ever!

The day that I went home before I actually got discharged, I saw the wound specialist. She was able to really clean out my incision superficially. When doing so, she noticed that the bottom of my wound was open as well as the top part. Every other nurse who had been cleaning my incision the past few days wasn't able to see that it was open because my hair was stuck in it- ummm gross. The nurse would cover it up with gauze, but it was in such an awkward spot that they put the tape on my hair and neck. It was so awkward and uncomfortable- then, when my neck moved at all, the tape would just fall off.

The wound care specialist had a great idea for keeping my wound covered- she suggested using a wide headband to hold the gauze in place instead of itchy and awkward tape. That's where my dad got the idea and went a little overboard- he went down to the gift shop of the hospital with my sister and literally cleared out the headband section. I can't say that I was mad about it though- options are always a good thing.

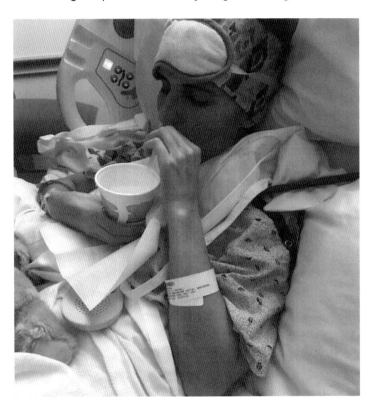

**ONE OF THE HEADBANDS THAT I WORE
TO KEEP THE GAUZE IN PLACE**

When we were finally discharged later that day on November 3, 2019, I was wheeled in a wheelchair out to the car. When I was wheeled past my roommate Elizabeth, she was crying. "May God bless you, baby. I will be praying for you," she said. What she said was really special to me. I feel like from the few days that I knew her, I was able to touch her heart. It meant a lot to me to have an impact on someone like that.

I was convinced that by the time that I left the hospital, I would finally be feeling better. Unfortunately, that wasn't the case. I still had horrible head pain and now, incision pain. Residents kept telling me to "wait it out" and "it will get better with time", but no one could tell me when it would get better. How much more time would I have to suffer? Literally, on our drive home from the hospital, I looked in the mirror and noticed that my tongue was coated with white. "Ew, do you see my tongue? What the hell is that?" I shrieked. "Oh boy- looks like thrush to me. Let me send a picture of that to Eliza", my mom said.

Sure enough, thrush it was. All of the antibiotics that I was on were the cause of it, so Eliza was able to call in a mouthwash for me to clear it up. Thank God for Eliza- seriously, what would we do without her?!

CHAPTER 14

Even though I was in pretty bad pain, I planned to start outpatient physical therapy and occupational therapy now that I was off of the steroids. I remember on my first day of outpatient physical therapy, we just did an evaluation that tested me on how much time it took me to get from point A to point B, my balance, etc. I had two physical therapists, both vestibular-certified, who would be working with me on my eyes as well. Afterwards, I had an evaluation with my occupational therapist, who also did a bunch of tests on me, testing the strength in my right arm and hand, my coordination, etc. As we were in the middle of one of the tests where I had to walk up the wall with my fingers, I burst out laughing again for no reason. I was kind of thinking about how awkward it was that she was just watching me slide my arm up a wall. What has my life come to? LOL.

"Oh my God, I'm so sorry. I have no idea why I laugh at inappropriate times. I'm so sorry," I said.

"It's okay," she said, "You don't have to explain yourself. Some of our patients do that, you don't have to be embarrassed by it."

Why the hell was I not able to control my emotions though?! I would cry at certain songs that I heard on the radio. Another example, I went to Verizon with my mom to get her phone fixed. The tech that was helping her was clearly bullshitting and had no idea what he was talking about, so I literally started laughing in the poor guy's face. I thought that maybe the surgery would fix my weird, uncontrollable emotions, but if anything, they were worse now. Over the next few weeks in therapy, I would have random outbursts of laughter in the middle of an exercise.

I remember one day as I was in the parking lot before therapy, my sister texted me the link to a video. Rebecca had been searching Dr. Brady almost daily because he said that he planned to publish my case, and by searching for him, she happened to come across a video of a girl named Elena who was around my age. In the video, she was being interviewed by the hospital where my surgery was too. She had a brain stem cavernoma resection like me that was also performed by Dr. Brady. Due to the crazy internet that we have at our fingertips, I was able to find Elena via social media and send her a message.

She got back to me almost instantly, and was so glad that I had reached out to her. Here I was thinking that I've found someone that I can talk to who can help me, but I quickly realized that I was helping her just as much. It's not everyday that you find someone around your age who had the same type of brain surgery as you, performed by the same surgeon.

My mom had been staying with Brandon and I to take care of me while I was recovering. One night, I was stupidly trying to get my sock on by standing and putting my foot up on a chair. I quickly lost my balance and my body slammed down onto the laminate floor. I felt my brain shake inside my skull. Being in pain before the fall happened definitely didn't help the fact that my head just got whiplash from my fall. At one point, we were told by a nurse that taking Advil was okay to take a certain amount of days after surgery. Advil can increase your risk of stroke, but since my cavernoma was removed, taking it was okay now. Advil worked a little better than Tylenol did so I wanted to try it to help take the pain away. It definitely didn't make the pain go away-more like took the edge off. For the next few weeks, I was taking Advil and Tylenol back and forth like candy around the clock to try to get ahead of my pain.

Another night when Rebecca came over, we were in a silly mood. Whenever my sister, mom and I were in one of those moods, it was over. We just cry laughing over the dumbest things. At one of my first big laughs, I noticed that I had really bad pressure and pain in my head. Rebecca kept making me laugh by making comments at the TV show we were watching. She was being freaking hilarious though. I kept asking her to please stop because my head would hurt really bad whenever I laughed. A couple of minutes later, she cracked another funny comment that made me laugh so hard that I couldn't catch my breath. To this day, I still remember what she said but I won't share it with you all because it was a bit inappropriate. Oh my God, the pain from that, I can't even explain it! "Rebecca, ya gotta go. Please. It hurts so much." I basically was like, "I'm sorry...I love ya... but don't let the doorknob hit you on the way out" and I kicked her out of my house LOL.

CHAPTER 15

After about eight full weeks of really bad pain, I finally felt like I was turning a corner. I mean, it was so bad. From the second my eyes opened in the morning, until I shut my eyes at night. Still pretty uncomfortable but the pain was finally becoming more bearable, and I could just start to really focus on my therapy without being so distracted by that.

Brandon and I had a small Christmas tree that I would decorate in our window every year for Christmas. This year, my mom surprised us with a full sized Christmas tree. I wanted to surprise Brandon and have it all set up for when he got home from work, so my mom and Rebecca helped me decorate it. We were blasting Christmas music, and my mom captured some videos of us dancing around while decorating the tree, although I danced super cautiously so that I wouldn't fall over.

On the day before Thanksgiving Eve, I woke up with a really bad stomach ache. I was doubled over in pain all day and I had no idea why. Maybe it was just that time of the month or something. Ever since I was taken off of birth control before my surgery, things had been very weird and irregular. On Thanksgiving

Eve, I had therapy. I made it through physical therapy and was in the middle of my occupational therapy session when the pain got really bad again in my stomach. I remember being on the arm bike telling my therapist that my stomach was hurting.

After my therapy session that day, my sister Rebecca picked me up to go to my mom and Mike's house for Thanksgiving. We usually switched off every year with my mom and dad, and this was my mom's year. With my dad, we usually went to upstate New York to our family's house. With my mom, we usually kept it pretty low-key and small. Especially with the past year that I was having, we just were keeping it to my mom, Mike, Rebecca and I.

It worked out that it was my mom's year because I wouldn't want anything else but to be low-key especially when I was not feeling the greatest. Rebecca and I called my mom in the car on our way to her house after therapy.

"My stomach is still really bothering me especially when I am moving around," I said on the phone.

"You know what, Rach- I think that maybe you should stop at an urgent care on your way here and make sure that it's nothing. I know how you are and I know that you will obsess over it for the next two days. A lot of places won't be open until next week after the holiday is over. Just get it checked out so you have peace of mind going into this weekend," she said.

It was only a thirty minute ride to their house, but I found an urgent care office that was right across the street from the hospital by my mom's house. My sister parked outside the front doors of the urgent care office and helped me walk in with my crutch. Once I sat down in the waiting area, Rebecca went back outside to park the car and came back in.

Rebecca went up to the desk for me and helped me sign in. We were the only ones in the waiting room at the time. Twenty minutes passed before I was called back to the exam room. Rebecca helped me walk and sat in the room with me. A nurse came in and did the basic screening questions for me- how tall are you, how much do you weigh, why are you here today, blah, blah, blah. "Thank you. The doctor will be in shortly," she said.

As I sat there waiting, I felt kind of silly because the pain went away. The pain was on and off all day. I didn't want to waste the doctor's time, but I also wanted to make sure that I had peace of mind before the holiday weekend so that I could relax. It wasn't very long before the doctor entered the room. He was six feet tall with glasses and messy gray hair. I told him the reason why I was there. He then pushed on different spots of my belly, asking me where it felt tender. When he pushed on the lower right side of my stomach, I winced in pain.

"There- that's exactly where the pain is," I said.

"Hmm," he said, "That's where your appendix is. I want you to go across the street to the emergency room to have them check it out for you."

Rebecca and I just kind of looked at each other like "are you kidding me? My appendix?!" Following the doctor's instructions, my sister helped me out of the office and back into the car. The hospital was just across the street so we didn't spend much time in the car. In those two minutes, I called my parents to let them know what was happening. They both insisted on meeting me in the emergency room.

Since we were just a short distance from my mom's house, she was able to get there as we were just checking in. We waited in the lobby of the emergency room for ten minutes before a nurse called my name to check me in. I vividly remember the admissions nurse- she was a heavier blonde woman dressed in bright blue scrubs, maybe in her late thirties. She was asking me basic questions about why I was coming in today, my prior history, etc. I showed her where my stomach was hurting.

"Yup. That looks like the appendix to me!" she said.

"Great, lady. Thanks for making me feel better," I thought to myself.

She brought me into my own room within the emergency room right away. I was expecting to be set up in the hallway again but I felt like a queen or something getting my own room right off the bat. I could get used to that. At that time, my dad showed up, so the three of them sat in chairs across from the stretcher that I was on. A doctor came in shortly after, who asked me to explain my symptoms to him again. "Ok. I'm going to order a CT scan of your stomach so we can see what's going on," he said. "You will need to drink barium sulfate contrast prior to the scan, so I'll order that now. That way, you can start drinking it. The sooner you finish it, the sooner we can order your scan."

Shortly after talking to the doctor, my nurse brought in two huge bottles of this orange concoction that they needed me to drink. It had to be close to a gallon.

"Don't worry hun, it doesn't taste that bad. I've heard it tastes like Tang. I brought you a cup of ice to chill it because I've heard it is easier to drink that way," she said. She wasn't lying. It wasn't HORRIBLE, it just wasn't something I'd want to voluntarily drink. And there was so much of it. My sister helped me get a system down- pour the orange drink into an empty cup, put some ice in the drink, chug it as quickly as possible, crunch on some ice chips as a chaser to the drink, then repeat. We did that about six or seven times until we finished the first bottle, just for reference.

It surprisingly didn't take long before I was taking my last sips of the second bottle. Before I knew it, I was being transferred to get my CT scan. "I can't believe I'm doing this for my stomach right now. I am barely getting over the fact that I just had brain surgery!" I thought. I don't remember much about how long we waited afterwards for my results of the scan. The doctor came back in to read them and I remember my heart pounding as I heard him start speaking to us- I can't afford a second surgery right now!!

"Good news and bad news," the doctor said. "The good news is that it's not appendicitis like we thought, and we will not need to operate. The bad news is that we found a cyst on your ovaries that is 7 by 4.7 centimeters. We need to get a better look at it though so I'm going to order an ultrasound of your ovaries to see if we can figure out what's going on," he said. Never a freaking dull moment with me. Was he joking or what? I was put on birth control at the age of thirteen to regulate my hormones. I was on it for years and years until September 19, 2019 where it was abruptly stopped when I was first admitted to the hospital.

Being on the pill for basically thirteen years and then being stopped so suddenly was probably not the smartest thing that I could have done for my body, but I had so many other things on my plate that this was the last thing on any of our minds. I was rolled into a room shortly after to get my ultrasound. A young woman was the tech. "Look, do you see that?" she said to me as she placed the wand over the painful spot on my stomach. "It's right there."

I tried to look up at the screen but it was positioned above me and looking up like that made me super dizzy. By her reaction, I knew that what we were dealing with had to be significant. "Alright," the doctor said as he looked over the results with us, "We're definitely seeing a cyst on your ovaries. The good news is that we will not have to do anything urgently. I strongly suggest that you see an endocrinologist to get this addressed as soon as possible though." I couldn't believe that:

> A. I knew something was definitely wrong (damn I am so in tune with my body though!)

> B. They actually found something that didn't have to urgently be addressed- I thought for sure they were going to have to cut me open...

I could see my whole family sigh with relief. "I just have to write up some of these notes and then we can start the discharge process," the doctor stated. Maybe about an hour later, we were discharged. At least I was being discharged and not admitted. Pulling into my moms house with my sister that night felt like the best thing to ever happen to me. I really thought that I was going to be admitted and sleeping in a hospital bed that night, but instead I'd be sleeping comfortably in my bed and better yet, the next day was Thanksgiving!

CHAPTER 16

Thanksgiving Day was so relaxing and low key. Just my mom, Mike, Rebecca and I enjoying time together, lounging in cozy clothes, eating some good ass Thanksgiving food! My stomach still hurt, but it's almost as if it hurt less knowing the cause and knowing that it would be addressed soon. It was a really nice Thanksgiving though. I had so much to be thankful for this year. I had the weekend off but on Monday, it was right back to work!

I was only doing physical and occupational therapy, but my mom was starting to notice that I was slurring my words a bit more than normal. The speech department at my rehab facility had a waitlist, but we were able to get an appointment for a consultation for that Thursday, December 5th since my therapists were able to squeeze me in. On Wednesday, December 4th, I remember waking up feeling really dizzy and off balance. My right hand felt a bit tingly too like pins and needles. Though I was feeling weird, I still went about my morning routine and prepared for my day of therapy. Before the start of each therapy session, my blood pressure would be recorded. On that day, it was abnormally low.

"Are you feeling okay?" My therapist asked me.

"I'm actually feeling pretty dizzy today to be honest with you," I said.

My physical therapist had a second therapist come over to my mat and check it again to make sure that the number was recorded correctly. It was still concerningly low, so they had me lay down flat on the mat. I just did some stretching and light exercise that day; nothing too vigorous to be cautious about the low blood pressure. When my occupational therapist came over to me for our session, which was right afterwards, she recorded my blood pressure again, which was still the same… super low. I mentioned to her that my right hand felt a little bit tingly too.

I don't remember exactly what I did with her that day, but I just have a clear memory of her telling me, "If your blood pressure is low like this tomorrow, you should go to the emergency room."

Later that day after therapy, the dizziness got worse. At one point, I got up to use the bathroom and I was stumbling and falling into the walls of the hallway as I made my way to the bathroom. The next morning, Thursday, December 5 2019, I woke up not feeling any better. Luckily, we had a blood pressure cuff at home so we were able to check it again. "It is still very low," my mom said, "I'm going to text Eliza to see what she wants us to do."

That was the morning that I was supposed to have my evaluation for speech therapy, so I started getting ready for the day so I wouldn't be late. We were seconds away from walking out of the door when we got a text back from Eliza. "Come to the emergency room here," the text read. I remember that drive to the emergency room so well. We weren't in a rush to get there at all. We stopped for gas and even went into the convenience store to get some snacks for the day. It's always a long day when I'm in the ER. We called the rehab center to apologize and cancel my speech evaluation for that day.

To be honest, this is where my timeline of events starts to get a bit confused and jumbled. While I was in the emergency room, I had an MRI scan to check for any changes to my brain. Both my mom and dad were with me that morning. Mike was away for the weekend, Brandon was working and Rebecca was in Boston for the weekend visiting friends. The MRI results showed that there was blood in my brain, but the emergency room doctors still believed that it was the same post-surgical residual blood that needed to be reabsorbed.

The doctors wanted to admit me to the neurology unit to monitor me for the night. Dr. Brady, my neurosurgeon, was actually in India at the time of my admission back into the hospital. He was ironically presenting a case study that he wrote about my surgery at a conference there. I do not remember much else about that Thursday night.

My mom slept on the recliner chair next to my bed, and my dad came back first thing on Friday morning. At some point on Friday during the day, an eye doctor specializing in neuro came to evaluate me. He came to my bedside with a briefcase full of equipment to test my eyes. After completing a few tests with a light, magnifying glass, and other random gadgets, he grabbed a paper napkin. He twisted the end of it until it formed a sharp point and poked the white part of my left eye. "Do you feel that?" he asked. "No, I don't feel a thing," I answered.

That was the first time I ever realized that my left eye had no feeling in it. He told me that it might be beneficial to get some prism lensed glasses eventually. I don't remember much else about that day, except for having some neurosurgery residents check in on me a couple of times. I told one of them about the

severe, throbbing pain in my head but he told me that I was going to have to be patient while my brain healed and maybe start
volunteering or something to take my mind off of the pain. Really
dude?? Volunteering to forget about the pain that I'm in?? That's
your response?? That comment made me so angry. I felt like he
was being ignorant AF. Why did nobody believe me?

He planned to discharge me to go home that Friday night.
My nurse from the day got the discharge note on her computer
though and declined it immediately. She then got on the phone
with the resident who planned to send me home. We heard her
on the phone in the hallway, "Listen, something isn't right. She's
not doing well- there is no way you are discharging her to go
home today," she said. Because of her pushback, I was kept at
the hospital again for the night- she won that one and I'm thankful that she did.

My memory of the evening was foggy, but I remember ordering ravioli with vodka sauce for dinner from the hospital menu.
Not going to lie, the menu was so big and actually really good.
After being admitted there so many different times, I knew what
was good on the menu and what should be avoided. About an
hour after I finished my dinner, I felt like I was going to be sick.
Luckily, my clutch mother grabbed a bucket just in time before
I threw up. Not to be gross, but it was a lot of vomit- like an abnormal amount of it. And usually when I got nauseous, I never
actually threw up. This time I did. And it was a shit ton. Maybe I
ate some expired raviolis, I thought.

I had a roommate that night who was in her seventies. I'm not
sure if she had dementia or something, but she was just super
confused. When it was time for bed, she started to freak out at
our nurse. There was an alarm under her mattress, so every time
that she tried getting up to "escape", it beeped and beeped until

the nurse came back in to turn it off. All of a sudden, I heard a loud thump on the other side of the curtain and the bed alarm was blaring again. She tried getting out of the bed again and fell on the floor this time. I then heard a ton of ruckus on the other side of the curtain. There were three or four nurses helping to lift her off of the floor and get her back into bed. Then, they wheeled her out of our room for the rest of the night. I don't know where they took her, but thank God because my ass could finally get a little rest.

In each hospital room, there was a private bathroom. In the middle of the night that night, I woke up to pee, using my crutch for assistance as I walked myself into the bathroom. As I was walking back to my bed, my right leg suddenly gave out from under me and I collapsed onto the floor.

My mom woke up from the loud thump that I made when I hit the ground. I couldn't get back up for some reason. My arms weren't holding my body weight to lift myself back up. My mom had to call my nurse into the room to assist with lifting me back up and getting me into my bed. I am not heavy at all so normally it'd be a breeze to get me up, especially with my assistance, but I remember not being able to assist them at ALL. I felt so weak and limp, like a wet napkin. Little did we know, that meaningless little walk to the bathroom and back would be my last walk.

CHAPTER 17

I woke up on Saturday, December 7, 2019 unlike any other morning in my entire life. I couldn't move the right side of my body from my neck all the way down to my toes. It was completely numb too. I don't know if I was starting to be "out of it" at that point but I wasn't scared by that feeling when I woke up. I don't know why. I think that maybe I assumed that it was happening because of the post-surgical blood and swelling. I really thought that it had just moved to a weird spot.

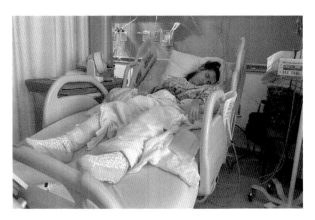

SLEEPING ON THE MORNING OF DECEMBER 7, 2019

I also woke up that morning feeling grateful for that nurse who fought for me to stay in the hospital one extra night because I couldn't imagine waking up at home like that. This is where things start to get really foggy for me. That Saturday, I was moved into a "cluster" room. This was a room that was one step below the ICU, but one step up from the room that I was originally in. It was a room that was closer to the nurses station where they were able to monitor me a lot closer and were required to check my vitals a lot more often.

At some point that Saturday, I stopped being able to urinate on my own. I had no feeling that told me when I had to pee, and I wouldn't have been able to pee even if I tried to. This required my nurse to do routine ultrasounds every few hours on my bladder. If she saw a certain amount of urine in my bladder, she had to catheterize me to empty out my bladder. I remember that it didn't hurt too much though- just a quick, little, uncomfortable pinch. Honestly, any other small details from this day as well as Sunday are hard for me to remember. I know that I was declining very rapidly, though.

They had been updating Dr. Brady about my status the whole time while he was in India. He tried to leave his conference early to fly home for the required medical attention that I needed but he ended up getting food poisoning while he was there and was not able to get on a plane. I really think that the neurosurgery team was trying to hold off on doing anything for as long as they could until Dr. Brady was back to operate on me but I was spiraling quicker than anyone had guessed and time was just running out. That Sunday night, I stopped being able to swallow my own saliva. My mom noticed it first because when I reclined back, I kept choking on my spit in my sleep.

I think that's when everybody knew that something had to be done and they had to do it without Dr. Brady. From India on Monday morning, Dr. Brady assigned one of his colleagues, Dr. Stevens, to take over my case in his absence. I definitely have a memory of meeting him. Dr. Stevens came into my room on Monday afternoon to greet us. "Hello, it's nice to meet you all," he said, "I've been in touch with Dr. Brady all weekend and know all about what's been going on in your case. The plan is that we are going to put you to sleep to do another MRI and we are going to intubate you. Depending on the results from the MRI, we will see if we need to operate on you again,"

At that point, I just wanted to say, "Do whatever the hell you gotta do to make me feel better, doc," but I didn't. What I really said was "Okay, so you're saying that you're going to put me to sleep and I won't know if I'm having surgery or not until I wake up either after an MRI or in the ICU after surgery? Will I definitely be asleep while I'm intubated the whole time? As long as I'm asleep and don't know that it's happening, I'll be fine," I said.

My mom, dad and Mike were there with me that morning. Mike returned home early from his trip to be with us. My sister returned from Boston the night earlier, but was at work. Brandon was at work too. After we heard what the plan was, we called Rebecca and Brandon to let them know that I was going to be intubated, possibly having surgery after. They both left work immediately and rushed over to the hospital to see me before I was put to sleep. I don't remember what time they put me to sleep on Monday but at some point in the afternoon, I was put to sleep and intubated. The reason why they had to intubate me before I even had the MRI was because I wasn't able to lay flat without choking on my spit. At least I think that's why...

The results of my MRI showed that I definitely required a second surgery. I really remember waking up and falling back asleep maybe two or three times while inside of the MRI machine. I was fighting anesthesia though so I was basically numb to any of my thoughts or my fears. Side note: my mom told me later on that they gave me the maximum dose of anesthesia but I was still fighting the whole time to wake up...I would. My second surgery was going to be the following morning- Tuesday, December 10 2019. They decided to keep me asleep after that MRI for the night though with the anesthesia.

My surgery the next morning took about six hours while family and friends waited anxiously in the waiting area. On the MRI the day prior to my surgery, it showed that there was either an infection in my brain or residual blood that could possibly be more of the cavernoma, but there was no way to tell for sure what they saw unless it was operated on and seen by the naked eye.

Dr. Stevens went into my brain through the same site as my original surgery which was behind my left ear. He verified to my family afterwards that the blood that everyone had been seeing on all of my scans was actually more cavernoma that was missed during my first surgery. After surgery was over, which was about 6:00 PM, I had a CT scan while I was still asleep. Dr. Stevens saw more blood on that CT scan which was worrisome to him because he wasn't sure if it was an active bleed or just post-surgical residual blood again.

Dr. Stevens ordered a repeat CT scan for 10:00 PM that night to check my brain again- if the blood that he saw stayed the same, it was okay. If he realized that there was new blood on the second scan when comparing it to the first one, he would have to operate on me again that night to find the source of the bleeding. I was asleep the whole time but he mentioned to my family that the bleeding could be coming from a specific artery. If that was the case and the artery was accidentally touched during the surgery, it could be fatal for me.

There was a lot of panic and fear from my family when hearing this information but they tried to stay as positive as they could. We aren't very religious or anything but they all went to the hospital's chapel that night to say prayers for me. Everyone in my family always tells me about this night and how it was probably the scariest night out of everything that has happened to me. Dr. Stevens was a great doctor, but he was very matter-of-fact and got straight to the cold hard facts. No sugar coating came from him. And that scared the shit out of them. At 10:00 PM that night, the CT was repeated. The results luckily came back to show evidence that there was only residual blood on my brain, not an active bleed. Since I had been asleep the whole day, the ICU doctors planned to wake me up the next morning. They knew that if they were to wake me up that night before the ventilator was removed, I would have gone ballistic. They also didn't want my blood pressure to spike because of stress and moving around too much. Can you blame me though?

That night, there was a major snowstorm, and my family was at the hospital so late since they were waiting for my second CT scan. Brandon went home for the night because he drove a truck that was good in the snow. The rest of my family booked a sketchy motel for the night next to the hospital. My mom needed some major convincing to stay at the motel instead of on a chair in the ICU waiting area, though. They convinced her that I would be asleep anyway and she might as well get a good night's sleep in a real bed for the night since it would be another long hospital stay for me.

The next morning before I woke up, my family sat down with Dr. Stevens in a conference room. He was very blunt and honest about what could be my reality when I woke up- it was something called locked in syndrome. This is when your whole body is paralyzed, but you are completely conscious and aware of what's happening around you. The only thing that I would be able to do is blink and move my eyes. He also told my family that the reason why I had been still bleeding prior to my second surgery was because the cavernoma that they thought was removed was actually still there a little bit; it was just hard to see and access. He believed that he got the rest of it this time, though.

Waking up in the ICU the next morning was a total trippppp. Imagine waking up to find out the news that you had a second brain surgery and it was two days later? I was trying to take all of the information in, but all I could really focus on was the fact that I still had a ventilator jammed down my throat, preventing me from being able to talk. I thought I was told that I wouldn't know about the ventilator?! I also immediately noticed that I was still paralyzed on my right side. I thought that the surgery would fix the fact that one side was a limp noodle, but I was paralyzed on my right side from the cavernoma bleeding in my brain prior to my surgery. The damage had already been done.

I remember waking up from the anesthesia twice the day prior- one time when I was in the MRI machine and one time as a woman was putting the ventilator in me. She had a short pixie haircut and she was hovering over me as I laid there. She was moving her hand with something from the left of my mouth to the right of my mouth, almost as if she was an artist, stroking a paintbrush onto my lips. I couldn't feel anything but I literally remember making eye contact with her like, "HELLO lady, I am awake and I don't really like that I know what is happening to me right now." I was in and out of consciousness for like five minutes during this process until they adjusted my anesthesia to a stronger amount. Traumatized is an understatement.

I could not believe that they would wake me up with a ventilator though. Were they out of their minds?! I already see PTSD in my future! I somehow got my sister to get me a piece of paper and a pen. I was then communicating with my family by writing with my left hand on the paper. You could imagine how that went- I could barely see a thing and I'm normally right handed. "I'm scared," I wrote. "I thought I would be sleeping," referring to the fact that I woke up with a ventilator down my throat and a feeding tube in my nose.

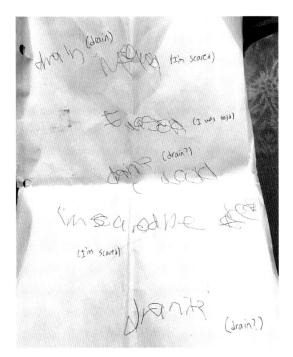

THE ACTUAL PIECE OF PAPER THAT I TRIED COMMUNICATING ON AND MY SISTERS ATTEMPT AT TRANSLATING MY WORDS

My memory is a bit fuzzy here so I'm not exactly sure how much time passed before they took my ventilator out. I gagged and coughed but it was over and out fairly quickly. Next to come out was the feeding tube in my nose. I had to have a speech therapist evaluate my swallowing first. Basically she had to see me eat and drink something and I needed to pass the test to have the feeding tube removed.

I was so worried that I would mess something up and not be able to get the feeding tube out. The therapist came in, and passed me with flying colors after seeing me eat and drink something. Ya girl's still got ittttt. "Okay, you did great Rachel! I just have to make sure that you are able to eat two more full meals before we take the tube out." I would like to think that I am a polite girl so I waited nicely until she left the room to go absolutely nuts. "I CANNOT HAVE THIS THING IN UNTIL AFTER LUNCHTIME!! ARE YOU KIDDING ME?! IT NEEDS TO COME OUT NOW. IT IS SO UNCOMFORTABLE."

I don't know what had come over me. I was just sooo agitated- it was so out of character for me to act that way. As I was going ballistic, Brandon's sister showed up to visit. She always coincidentally came at my worst moments! "Rach, relax. Say hi," Rebecca said. Mad as hell, I was like. "Hi." But then I continued to lose my shit. I was just so uncomfortable. Rebecca then turned to her, saying, "This probably isn't the best time. I would meet up with your brother and come back in a little while."

She then met up with Brandon and their mom who were both at the hospital visiting me but had just gone out to get some lunch. I'm not that kind of person at all, but I will admit that I was having a complete meltdown. She came back with Brandon after I had calmed down a little bit, though and I was feeling better. It was so nice whenever she came to visit me. I have always looked at her like my little sister- It's nice to know that I was so important to her too. I always said that aside from being Brandon's sister, she was one of my best friends.

Tuesday, Wednesday, and Thursday passed by and I was still in the ICU. I don't have much memory of those days, but I remember being extremely tired and in so much pain. I was able to make it through with no painkillers again, only Tylenol. I really wanted to avoid taking them if I could. I remember physical therapists coming in the room to work with me, but always at the worst times, just as I was about to nap or something. I couldn't move much at all, so they would tell me to push my knee into the bed as a strengthening exercise for my quad muscle.

The other thing that I remember is that my nurse would always try to get me to sit in the chair next to my bed so I wasn't lying in the same spot in bed all day. For me to be able to sit up in a chair, my nurse would have to call a second nurse into the room. They would roll me onto my side, put a bright green and yellow harness under me, latch the harnesses to attachments on the ceiling, and literally hoist me into the air and carry me to get to the chair. I HATED that thing- moving at all hurt my head so bad and made the room spin.

I don't remember what day of the week it was, but as soon as Dr. Brady made it home from India, he was in the ICU by my side making sure that I was okay. I was also put back under his care as my doctor. That Sunday was one of the last NY Giants games of the football season, and Eli Manning's last game of his career. Even though I couldn't really see much, I tried to watch every snap.

A few months earlier after my first surgery, my friend Ethan had Eli send me a video saying that the Giants wished me the best in my recovery and that they were all hoping and praying for me. Eli won his last game as a Giant that day, his last ever game. I was literally crying so much. I don't know why- I think I was just sad to see him retire and emotional that he as well as my friends from the Giants sent me a ten second video- a simple gesture that truly made me feel so happy and loved.

By the end of the week, I was still in the ICU. I was still not able to see the television very well, but would try to watch it in between my naps. I remember seeing a commercial at one point for pepperoni pizza at some nasty chain restaurant and I couldn't get the thought out of my head after that. I have no idea why because I never ordered pepperoni on my pizza and I especially never ordered pizza from chain restaurants (I'm from Jersey for God's sake) but I just needed to have it. My dad went out one day to get a pie for us. He loved doing that kind of stuff for my sister and I. I just remember eating a greasy pepperoni pizza that evening with my sister while in the ICU after my second major surgery. Can you picture it?

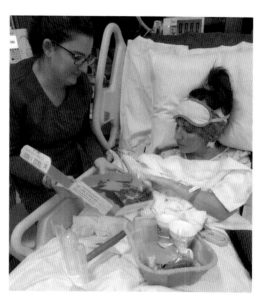

That pizza was a significant part of my story. I didn't know it at the time, but my mom noticed that as I was eating the pizza, I was struggling to swallow it. If you ask me, it was probably because it was so delicious and I was inhaling it quicker than my brain would let me swallow it. The next day, my dad brought in a letter that he received from my grandma's sister. In the letter to my father, it contained a prayer, which instructed him to read it aloud to me while throwing salt over my head. Most of the prayer was in another language- Turkish maybe? I kid you not, he showed up to the ICU that day with the prayer and a plastic bag filled with salt, and threw it over me while he read the prayer aloud.

The next day was Friday, December 20- I was supposed to be released and transferred to a new hospital for rehab (my sister worked as a speech therapist at that hospital and because I had a bad experience during my first time at rehab, we felt more comfortable sending me to a new hospital). As the day progressed though, my mom and dad were feeling increasingly uneasy about sending me to start rehab. I was very groggy and just not myself. I was also starting to taper off of the steroids again, and could barely hear a thing- my head and ears felt like they were filled up with fluid. My left ear was deaf after the first surgery, and now my right ear was muffled.

My parents didn't think I was ready to be sent off to rehab just yet and talked to Dr. Brady about keeping me in the hospital through the weekend and transferring me that Monday. Dr. Brady was okay with whatever we were comfortable with, so he cleared out a double room on the neurology unit so that my mom could stay with me and sleep in an actual bed (she wasn't allowed to stay overnight with me in the ICU, so she would sleep on a bench in the ICU waiting area every night).

Before our room was ready, my dad went to an Asian restaurant in town to grab us dinner. I ordered chow fun (a thick noodle dish because I started to realize that I was having some trouble swallowing too and I thought that a thicker noodle would be easier for me to eat). What did he come back with? Mei fun aka the thinnest noodle dish on planet earth. Basically angel hair- They gave him the wrong thing by mistake.

I figured that I would try it anyway, so my mom put some into a styrofoam cup for me to eat. I took one bite and all of the thin noodles immediately stuck to the back of my throat. I was coughing for a good couple of minutes to get them out. Something felt off- maybe my brain was just recovering from the surgery and confused. Also, I just assumed that it could be due to the swelling from tapering off of my steroids again. All of the ICU doctors were saying that once I was up and moving in rehab, things would start to get better for me and I would start to feel better.

Later that evening, I was moved up to the neurology unit to the room that Dr. Brady had arranged for us. I basically knew all of the nurses and techs by then, but I grew extremely close with one nurse, Clarisa. She was close to my age, and was just so sweet and caring. As soon as they wheeled me upstairs, I saw Clarisa and immediately burst into tears. She wasn't assigned to be my nurse but she was helping to wheel me into my room. It hit me at that point as to what had happened to me. Clarisa was on vacation when I first got admitted this time around, so the last time that I saw her, I was walking, and now I was paralyzed on my right side, not even able to roll over in bed. She told me that she was going to come to my room when her shift was over. She ended up staying with me after her shift for almost an hour, just talking. She was such a sweetheart- it made my night to hang with her.

Napping didn't help my exhaustion. I felt like I was in a cloud. I couldn't even stay awake for the nurse's shift change at 7:00 PM, where my new nurse came to give me my evening medicine. My mom woke me up at around 8:30 PM, when the nurse was in my room to give me my pills. I legit couldn't hear a thing- it was getting worse and worse by the minute. We had to crush all of the pills in pudding, and as you can imagine, waking up from being asleep to eat chemical flavored chocolate pudding was not exactly what I would call a "fun time".

Saturday night and Sunday night were the same deal. I couldn't stay awake so my mom would tell me to go to sleep and just wake me up when my nurse came around with my medicine. Sunday night during my sleep, I heard my mom calling my name and felt her tapping me on the shoulder to wake me up. I can't even explain it well but it felt like my body wouldn't allow itself to wake up. It was such a scary feeling. It felt like my whole body was paralyzed and I was stuck in my sleep- I couldn't control my own body to get out of the sleep that I was in. Then, when I woke up, I couldn't use my voice or speak at first. My mom asked me what was wrong but I wasn't able to answer her. I'll never forget that night because the feeling was terrifying and indescribable.

CHAPTER 18

Monday, December 23 was the day that I was transferred to rehab. We felt comfortable being at that hospital because my sister worked there. Before I was transferred, Elena, the girl from the video who had the same surgery and surgeon as me, came to visit. I really didn't feel well, but I really wanted to meet her. When she arrived, she sat next to my bedside to the right of me (which was my good ear). She couldn't have been any closer to my bedside, but I could barely hear anything she said to me unless she screamed it in my ear. It was so nice of her to come meet me though and share her story with my family and I. I am sure that it brought my family a lot of comfort too knowing that she was once in my position, and now, she was driving, graduating college and becoming a nurse.

I don't remember the ambulance ride while being transferred to rehab, but I remember being wheeled into my room when I got there. A nurse was talking to me as soon as I arrived in my room but I wasn't able to see her because my vision was so wavy. "You're Rebecca's sister, right? Welcome! You're in great hands here with us." I had a beautiful single room that overlooked the river. It was a shame because I couldn't even turn my head to look out the window and take in the view. My mom told me how beautiful and tranquil it was, but it was so blurry and made me dizzy to even try looking outside.

My first evening dinner was ground turkey, chopped up green beans and cranberry sauce. Even though the food was chopped up, I was really having a difficult time swallowing it. It kept getting stuck in my throat. My dad went down to the cafeteria to find me something easier to eat. We could always count on him for spoiling me with some food. He came back upstairs with banana cream pie and I wasn't upset about it...Dessert for dinner? Sureeee! I had a hard time swallowing that too, though, but managed to get it down with sips of Ensure in between bites (since I wasn't eating a lot and getting the best nutrition, I drank a ton of Ensure...chocolate flavor of course).

At that point, I still wasn't able to pee or tell when I had to pee, so my nurse had to scan my bladder and catheterize me a few times throughout the day. The next day was Christmas Eve and my first official day in therapy. I felt like my brain was totally foggy, and I could barely see anyone or hear anything. I didn't know this but apparently my sister made a sign that hung over my bed that read, "Hard of hearing- Please come to the right side of the bed and speak loudly." I was kind of just...there. Not really contributing to conversation or anything. It was now Christmas Eve. I had occupational therapy first, and the therapist's plan was to first move me from my bed to a chair by the window.

She planned to help me change out of my hospital gown into some normal clothes. She had to call a tech into the room to hold me once I sat up to make sure that I didn't fall over the edge of the bed. I couldn't even sit up anymore. I don't know how they managed to get me to the chair, but all I remember was being thrown around like a freaking rag doll to that chair. I am still really traumatized from that. My torso was like a wet noodle, totally unable to support my body weight whatsoever. Every time they would move me gently, it felt like my body was being whipped around violently. What a horrific experience- literally horrific. On top of that, I couldn't really hear or see them. My voice was also becoming really weak. The therapist asked me what I did for work. When I tried to answer her, what came out of my mouth was incomprehensible. What I tried to say sounded nothing like what actually came out of my mouth. It took so much power for me to try and use my voice- why was this happening? I could only get a few words out before my voice faded away to nothing. We all just thought that this was a symptom of being tapered off the steroids again and things would get worse before they got better again because now I was two surgeries in.

I kept randomly getting the feeling of pins and needles in my left hand that day too. I was terrified because the last time I had that feeling in my right hand, I woke up paralyzed the next day. I kept turning to my family and saying, "Numb. Tingling" over and over again. I showed them that it was the feeling that was coming from my left hand now. I knew that they understood what I was saying, so I was trying to say as little as possible so that I could preserve my voice. After occupational therapy was over, I was moved back to my bed for physical therapy. Pillows had to support my trunk on both sides, otherwise I would just fall over to one side.I couldn't even sit up straight.

I remember staring in the therapist's eyes, so sleepy that I could pass out at any second. She was basically just moving and stretching my legs from the bed because Lord knew I was not moving again. I don't remember talking to her at all, but I remember the gray zip up sweatshirt that she wore over her green scrubs. That vision is still very clear in my head. After PT and OT were over, I had my speech evaluation. The speech therapist wanted to see what I was able to eat to determine what diet I should be on. I was currently on a chopped diet and nectar thick liquids. She kept me on that diet, however, she told me that I was able to take little sips of normal water if I was being supervised and didn't cough when I drank it. My family was extremely worried about the symptoms that I was having and although we were all thinking that it was from the steroids, they wanted to do another CT scan to just make sure everything was okay. The CT was completed that day and it showed that I still had residual blood, but no new changes from that.

The night of Christmas Eve is another night clear in my mind that I will never forget. The nurses got an order from one of my doctors to give me this nasty ass drink that tasted like expired Mountain Dew. My mom was with me of course (she basically had to be with me night and day at that point because I couldn't do anything by myself anymore). She tried to make me drink it through a straw even though I could barely even smell it without gagging.

The speech therapist gave her this tasteless powder that dissolved into any liquid to make it nectar thick, so that it would be easier for me to get down. My mom put the powder in the nasty drink and promised me that if I was able to get the whole drink down, I could have some water afterwards. Even just a small sip of water sounded like pure heaven to me.

Every nasty sip of this drink was one sip closer to a blissful cup of ice water. I had such a hard time drinking that stuff, but knowing that water would come shortly afterwards made it a little easier to drink it. It took me an estimated twenty five minutes to get an eight ounce bottle down. Not only did I not like the taste, but I had a really tough time swallowing it even though it was thickened and should have been "easier" for me to drink. We called my nurse back in the room afterwards to ask for a cup of ice water, as promised. I'm pretty sure I grabbed the water out of my nurse's hands before she even had the chance to hand it to me- I was so thirsty!

I knew that I was struggling so I had to take my time taking very small sips. I was just dying for water like never before. On the first tiny little sip that I took, it slipped down my throat before I was able to swallow, and I started to cough. I tried a second sip and the same thing happened- it slid so fast. "That's it," my mom said, "No more water. I don't want you choking Rach." That cup of water meant everything to me though. It may sound dumb, but at the time, it was all that I could think about- knowing that I couldn't drink it made me want it more. I felt the most parched I had ever felt in my entire life. I was on a new medication too that gave me dry mouth, especially at night, so I was dying for water. Mustering up enough energy to get any words out was starting to become really difficult.

"I deserved that! You promised!" I said.

"I know Ray but you keep choking on it. Here, let's try some of this," she said as she opened up a container of nectar thick lemon water.

I took one sip and almost vomited. The taste of thickened water with artificial lemon flavoring was nasty AF, and it didn't satisfy my need to have regular water at all. I'd rather have nothing than have nectar thick artificial lemon water. She wouldn't give me normal water though- I thought she was being such a bitch. I felt deceived and was so pissed. At that point, it was almost 11:00 PM. The nurse came back in to check on me and I grabbed her hand. "Please!! Water?" I pleaded. She looked to my mom as if she needed her permission to let me try it again. "Go ahead," my mom said, "But Rachel- if you choke one more time, that's it."

The nurse left the room to get some ice water again. When she came back to my room, I took a deep breath and thought to myself, "Okay, focus Rach. This is your last chance." She handed me more water and on the first sip, it slipped down again too quickly, prompting me to cough. "Alright Rachel, you're done. No more water tonight. I'll be happy to give you the thickened lemon water if you want it, otherwise we're going to sleep now. I don't want to hear about water anymore." I remember being so beyond angry, but didn't really have the energy to fight back anymore. My doctor prescribed me a spray that moistened my mouth to help with the dry mouth, so I took one spritz of it and went to bed for the night. What a Christmas Eve.

Waking up on Christmas morning was anything but normal. No tree, no presents, no yummy breakfast, no celebrating. Just a hallway of beeping monitors, chatting nurses and my mom sleeping at my bedside on the recliner chair. I wanted to look out of my window so badly on Christmas morning, but I couldn't turn my head. Even if I could, I wouldn't have been able to see shit. I woke up with the most horrible dry mouth I have ever experienced, still craving water just as bad as I did the night prior. As the morning progressed, my family started to trickle in. Dad, Mike, Rebecca, Brandon.

When they walked in, all I could do was point to my mom and say, "Liar! She's a F'in liar!" I was still so pissed at the fact that she promised me water and then took it away from me. I just needed something to hydrate me. I thought to myself and promised to myself that I would never ever take water for granted when I was able to drink it again. I would never leave a glass of water full at a restaurant ever again. My dad had a great idea- maybe I could try an ice pop. The only requirement that I gave him was no cherry flavor though.

When I was little, I ate a bunch of cherry airheads after the movies and then threw them all up. Now I'll never eat anything cherry flavored again- it kind of traumatized me. An hour later, my dad arrived back at my room, holding a red ice pop. Since it was Christmas, the supermarket was closed and he had to go to a convenience store. They only had cherry flavored ice pops... My freaking luck. I felt like I was just there, laying in the bed, totally hopeless and unable to move, or hear, or see. I felt like I was withering away. Dad also bought me an orange Gatorade at the store. Since I had the powder that made drinks into a nectar thick liquid, I was allowed to put that in Gatorade and I was so excited. My energy, particularly my voice, was even worse than the day before.

The first time that I noticed it was really bad was when Brandon was leaving the hospital to go to his dad's house for Christmas. He leaned over the bed to give me a kiss and I remember trying to say to him,

"Don't go." I was scared about everything that was happening to me and wanted him to stay with me.

"What?" he said, "I can't understand you, Rach."

"Don't go." I tried to say again, reaching for his hand.

"Rachel, we can't understand what you're saying," my mom said. "Brandon's leaving to go see his dad. Give him a hug and a kiss goodbye."

That moment was a memory that I constantly flash back to. It was so horrible. Talking, but not being able to be heard. Imagine trying to speak, but nobody is able to understand you. It sounds like a scary dream, but it was my reality. What the hell was happening to me? I was so scared. Brandon left, and later that Christmas day, my sister and dad had their chairs pulled up next to my bed. Rebecca was holding a cup filled with nectar thick grape juice and handed me a straw. With the straw, I'm pretty sure that I was able to get the whole thing down fairly quickly. Shortly afterwards though, I got the urge that I was going to vomit again.

"Bucket," I mumbled and pointed to it. Luckily, Rebecca was able to understand what I said just in time. I grabbed the bucket out of her hands and threw up so much that it filled up the entire bucket tray and overflowed a little bit onto her leggings. Projectile vomit was an understatement. Merry Christmas Rebecca- that was my gift to you, sis LOL. After throwing up, I felt even more sick and weak. I threw up everything that was left in my body. Now, I had nothing for my body to burn its energy on because I really wasn't eating anything at that point. One of the doctors that was on call came to see me that evening and decided to put me on an IV drip for fluids. Also, all of my medication was going to be administered through the IV as well because I wasn't able to swallow my medication, let alone swallow water. What a merry Christmas it was.

December 26 was my dad's birthday. At that point, whenever I would try to speak, no sound would come out at all. My sister's supervisor came to see me that morning, realizing that I had no way to communicate now. I couldn't talk, hear, or see very well at that point. She brought me a clipboard with a printout of the alphabet on it and gave it to me to use as a way of communicating. I would point to each letter to spell out different words. I couldn't use my right side so I couldn't hold the board with one hand and use my other to point to a letter. I had to rest the board on my lap when pointing to the letters. When my dad finally showed up to my room, the first thing that I did was spell out, "H-a-p-p-y b-i-r-t-h-d-a-y"

He lit up. It looked like he was going to cry and he told me thank you. My sister later told me that wishing him a happy birthday meant so much to him. He was happy that I remembered it was his birthday- that I was even aware of what day it was. I don't remember when but at some point that day, speech therapists came to my room to evaluate my swallowing again. This time, Brandon happened to be in the room with me. The first thing that they gave me was a spoon full of yogurt. I remember holding the yogurt in my mouth, but not being able to swallow it. My brain didn't let me. "Come on Rach, do it for me. I know you can do it Rach," Brandon was encouraging me.

I tried so hard, but I legitimately couldn't swallow it. YOGURT. I couldn't swallow yogurt. My family could also tell that I had secretions in the back of my throat but my body didn't have enough power to cough and clear my throat now. "Come on, Rachel- COUGH!" they all would yell at me. I could tell that they were frustrated but I really couldn't muster up a cough to clear my throat. When I tried, out came a measly little sound, nothing close to an actual forceful cough. As a result, my mom or my nurse would literally have to suction out the back of my throat with a little vacuum thing. As a result of not being able to cough or swallow saliva, I wasn't able to lay down flat in bed.

Because I hadn't eaten anything in a few days and wasn't able to swallow at all now, the doctors discussed and decided to schedule a procedure for me to get a PEG feeding tube put in. That is the tube that goes directly into the stomach. I was basically a vegetable at that point, and nobody knew that I knew what was going on anymore, except for me. I knew exactly what was happening the whole time, but couldn't talk to anyone, see anything or hear anything. Funny story: Rebecca's fiancé's mother had been sending Rebecca with home cooked meals to bring me. She always KILLED the eggplant parm and she knew that I loved it so much. I realized that it had been in the hospital refrigerator for a couple of days now and I wasn't going to be able to eat it anytime soon. I pointed on the board to try to say, "F-r-e-e-z-e t-h-e e-g-g-p-l-a-n-t"

God forbid the freaking eggplant went to waste. It was too good to waste honestly. My mind was totally there, but my physical being wasn't. That night, I had taken pain medication for the first time ever. The pain was so intense and Tylenol wasn't going to cut it. I still got the crazy sensitivity to medication where my tongue and/or lip would swell up but now that I wasn't able to talk and express what was happening, it made things a lot scarier for me.

Just prior to taking the painkiller, I was saying a bunch of dumb shit on the board, about the eggplant for example. It was frustrating to my family to understand what I was saying because I couldn't see very well so every time I would point to a letter on the board, my finger would be pointing in between four letters. Out of frustration, which I totally understand because I'd probably do the same, my mom finally said, "Okay, that's it. Enough with the damn board already!" and grabbed it from me to place on the window sill so I would shut up. I wanted to say "Wait, wait, wait! One more thing!" but wasn't able to speak so all that I could do was signal to her the number one to show that I had one more thing to say. She gave me the board back and I wrote, "M-y t-o-n-g-u-e i-s s-w-o-l-l-e-n."

I vividly remember my sister being the first one able to make out what the hell I was saying. Her and my mom rushed to get my nurse in the room to put Benadryl through my IV. On Friday,

December 27, a gastroenterologist was scheduled to come evaluate me to discuss the PEG tube procedure that I was going to have. I really don't remember this day so much but I was told that I took the same medication again for pain. Shortly afterwards, my mom called the nurse to come suction my throat because I was making gurgling noises. As my nurse was trying to put the suction in my throat, the tube no longer fit in and I was turning blue. My nurse called for help and a rapid response team was there in seconds. I remember having like ten doctors/nurses around my bed, hovering over me. From my perspective, I thought that I had been napping and next thing I knew, a million people were around me. The truth is, my nap was probably me passing out from anaphylactic shock. I was really confused.

They injected a steroid in my IV which reversed the reaction that I was having and gave me an oxygen mask to get my breathing back under control. For rapid responses, they announce it over the whole hospital's loudspeaker saying what floor the rapid response was being called on. My sister was working in the hospital that day and heard the announcement over the loudspeaker. I was in really bad shape at that point so she heard the announcement and automatically knew that it was for me when she heard what floor it was on. She called my mom who was outside of my room with Mike. My mom was obviously very shaken up by the whole thing. My sister then quickly ran up to my floor to be with them while the doctors tended to me.

My dad was in the hospital too but was hanging out in the lobby at the time- he was waiting for the gastroenterologist to come in for my consultation. My sister called my dad right away and told him to come up to my room. She told him that the rapid response that was announced on the hospital speaker was for me. As all of the doctors were crowding around my bedside, the gastroenterologist happened to come into my room for the consultation. He was confused by what was going on. "I'll come back at another time," he said.

At that point, one of the doctors that was in my room looked my mom in the eyes and said, "You have to get her back to the hospital where her surgery was. We can't give her the help that she needs here." Truly, I thank God for that doctor because I think she might be the reason why I'm alive today.

CHAPTER 19

I remember the ambulance crew coming into my room to transfer me back to the hospital where Dr. Brady was. The medics that came to transport me were two men and a woman. One of the men was driving the ambulance and the other man was sitting in the back behind my stretcher. The woman was beside me in the back, next to my stretcher. My mom and sister talked to them prior to the ride, because they wanted to make sure that they had equipment to resuscitate me just in case I collapsed on the ride back to the hospital. I was really that bad. I remember the woman that was next to me in the ambulance was watching me like a hawk, and urged me to raise my hand if I felt like I needed to be suctioned or anything.

I was delusional and basically just fell asleep the whole ride in the ambulance. It was after 7:30PM at that point and it was about a forty minute drive from where we were. When I arrived back at the hospital, I was immediately placed back in the intensive care unit. I was so out of it- I just remember the nurse introducing herself to me as I was fighting to stay awake. That's it. It was around 9:30 PM.

My mom, dad and sister were in the ICU room with me, where the doctors told them that they were taking me for an MRI ASAP. I normally would need a Xanax or something to get me through the MRI, but I was so sleepy and loopy that I think I slept through the whole thing. I don't even remember getting an MRI. The results weren't going to be read until later that night or early the next morning, so my dad went home and my mom and my sister slept on the benches in the intensive care unit waiting area.

Every morning, the ICU doctors completed rounds where they would visit with each patient or their families. My mom told me that all of the ICU doctors were acting very sheepish that morning when they got to my room. My sister said that she remembered that they weren't making eye contact with her either. When my mom and sister asked if my MRI results were back yet, they responded by saying, "Dr. Brady wants to come in and read you the results himself."

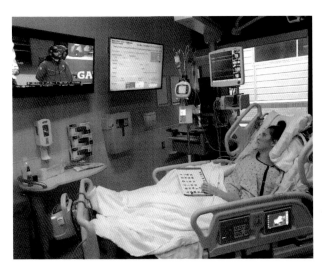

IN THE ICU WITH MY COMMUNICATION BOARD

A short time later, Dr. Brady called my mom's cell phone to tell her that the results of the MRI showed that my brain was swollen, very swollen, and he wanted to have a meeting with my family to see what my options were going to be. Like the night prior, I was sleeping basically all day, and don't really remember a thing. Family and friends came to visit me that day, but I have no recollection of it.

My large, extended family created a group text at the time, sending each other updates as they got any information about me. They decided to coordinate a group prayer for me. At exactly 9:30 PM that night, they all stopped what they were doing and said a prayer for me. I never realized what the power of prayer could do for somebody until I was the one who needed it the most.

Sunday, December 29, 2019 was the day that Dr. Brady came to meet with my family. They went into a meeting room in the ICU to discuss his thoughts. He said that my MRI showed that the swelling had gotten worse and I had something called hydrocephalus aka a large build-up of fluid. He told my family that it was very serious and he wasn't going to sugarcoat anything. He told them that they could choose the "watch and wait" approach to see what happens with me but I would potentially just stay the way that I was and never get better.

The other option was that he could perform what he called a "Hail Mary" surgery, one last effort, to go in through the back of my head to my brain stem to find the bleeding source. He said going through the back of the head was extremely dangerous and risky but it might be the angle that was needed to see more that they weren't able to see from the original surgery site. My whole family agreed that they wanted to take the risk and have him perform a third surgery, but Dr. Brady insisted on discussing it with me first so I could make the decision myself.

It's really crazy because I don't remember much from Friday or Saturday or even Sunday, but I remember what happened when Dr. Brady came into my room that day. My breathing, voice and swallowing weren't working correctly but I was fully aware cognitively and capable of making my own decision about this. My family decided that they all didn't want to come into the room at once to overwhelm me, so my sister and mom were the only two who accompanied Dr. Brady.

I remember seeing him wheel in a little machine to show me what my MRI showed. He then explained the options to me and handed me my communication board to answer. Without hesitation, I automatically pointed to the words, "I w-a-n-t i-t o-u-t." Then, he said, "You tell me when you want this surgery; do you want to have it right away or wait a few days?" I pointed to my board again, "R-i-g-h-t a-w-a-y" I said. He literally cleared his entire schedule for me, and scheduled my surgery for the first thing on Monday morning.

I was woken up very early in the morning on that Monday, December 30, 2019 by my nurse in the ICU to prepare me for surgery. She was helping me change into a new hospital gown. I couldn't even sit up so I had to roll over onto one side and have her untie my old gown. She then helped me roll onto my right side. Almost immediately, the sudden movement to my right side made me throw up all over the bed and down the side of the bed to the floor.

It's almost like my body gave me no warning that it was going to happen, I just threw up everywhere. Because of the hydrocephalus that I had, it was making me throw up insane amounts at a time. Hydrocephalus is a buildup of fluid deep within the brain and it's ventricles. The fluid put a lot of pressure on my brain which was causing the sleepiness and large amounts of vomiting. My mom came into my room as they were cleaning up the vomit and I pointed to the communication board so that she could grab it for me. "T-e-l-l D-r B-r-a-d-y I t-h-r-o-w u-p" I pointed.

I remember saying that- I was so adamant about it because my fear was that I'd be lying flat on the surgical table and choke on my own throw up. Thinking back to that now, it doesn't make any sense because he was going to go through the back of my head, meaning that I would be on my stomach anyway, but I guess I wasn't really thinking clearly at that time anymore.

I don't remember saying goodbye to my family before surgery, but I remember waiting in the operating room holding area with my mom and my dad. I was basically a total vegetable, unable to talk, unable to feel when I had to use the bathroom, unable to eat or drink, swallow, hear, move, see etc. The only thing I could do at that point was breathe. Miraculously, all of a sudden, in the OR holding area, I felt the sudden urge to pee. And I had to go… really, really, really bad. For weeks prior to that, I never had the feeling to go at all, and now, it just so happened that while I was about to go into a life or death surgery, I had the feeling. WTF?

On my communication board, I told my parents that I had to pee. It was a really strong feeling. My parents were probably like, "Really, Rachel??? Now?? What great timing" but I don't remember what their actual reactions were. I would guess that they were probably happy that I even felt the urge to use the bathroom at all. My mom walked away to notify one of the nurses for me. The feeling was getting stronger and stronger, and waiting for a nurse to come felt like it was unbearable. I was honestly about to pee in my pants. Finally, the nurse came in with a bedpan so I could urinate.

When the bedpan was in place, I tried to pee. But nothing came out. I couldn't relieve the feeling. What the hell, it was so strange because the feeling was stronger than I have ever felt in my entire life. Shortly afterwards, Dr. Brady was ready to prep me for surgery, meaning I had to say goodbye to my parents, and also leave my communication board behind. All I could think about was having to pee though. I don't even remember saying goodbye to my parents. I just remember my mom telling me that they would catheterize me once I was asleep before they started surgery and I would pee then.

I was wheeled into the operating room, where I remember seeing about six people in the room wearing blue scrubs, including Dr. Brady. I wasn't afraid. I honestly wanted to get put to sleep so badly so that they could catheterize me and I could finally pee. It felt like I was going to pee in my pants or my bladder was going to explode in my body but I was not able to talk to communicate that to anyone. I grabbed one of the OR assistant's hands and traced the word "P-E-E" over and over again in his palm to try to make him understand that I was about to explode and wanted to go to sleep ASAP. He clearly didn't understand what I was doing and probably thought that I was a nut. I guess I can look at that feeling as a blessing because I was so preoccupied with having to pee that I wasn't even thinking about the fact that I might be put to sleep and never wake up. That thought didn't cross my mind a single time. That's the last thing I remember.

My family told me that my surgery lasted between four and six hours. Afterwards, Dr. Brady came out of the operating room to speak with my family about the surgery. He told them that it looked like a bomb had gone off in my brain stem and that there were blood clots EVERYWHERE. My brain stem was extremely swollen and it was on the verge of exploding too but he got every single blood clot out from there. He was able to tell that I had five brain bleeds or "strokes" because the color of each bleed was slightly different based on the age of the blood. He also told my family that he found more cavernoma that wasn't visible from the initial two surgeries because it could only be seen from a different angle. It's not like you can just go into someone's brain stem and start moving things around to look for the cav. They had to be extremely cautious each time to make sure that they did not cause major brain damage. I was still sedated but I was moved to a room in the intensive care unit that day.

They didn't know how I was neurologically affected by the surgery until they did the neurological tests on me. They had taken some of the sedation away from me that day so that Dr. Brady could complete his neurological testing, but still had enough sedation so I could be asleep. The signs were good after surgery, but only time could tell how I would progress. The real test would be when I actually woke up.

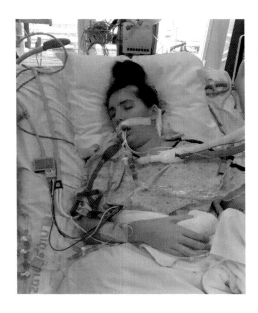

The intensive care unit doctors fought to keep me asleep for the night because whenever they lightened the sedation on me, I would become agitated because I was uncomfortable with the ventilator and the feeding tube. All I could say now about that is thank God that they kept me asleep. My heart rate and blood pressure would just skyrocket whenever they lightened the sedation at all. My family told me that whenever Dr. Brady was near the ICU the rest of that day, he would stop by my room to check on me. It had to be at least three or four times that day they told me. Everyone was just so happy that I made it through the surgery alive.

The next day was December 31, 2019, New Years Eve. I was still sedated, with a breathing tube and feeding tube in. I was taken for an MRI, with a respiratory technician by my side. The ventilator machine was disconnected from me as I was wheeled into the hallway and the technician had a manual air bag that he used to push air through my lungs to assist me with breathing. Every fifteen to twenty seconds, he would squeeze the bag that was connected to the tube down my throat, like a balloon.

Push the elevator button. *Squeeze.* *Walk down the hallway a little.* *Squeeze.* My mom told me that it was absolutely horrifying to watch that. Her daughter, getting wheeled down the hallway unconscious on a stretcher, with a man that was squeezing a plastic balloon every once and a while to push air through her lungs. She was unable to tell if those squeezes were the only way that I was able to breathe or not.

After my MRI was over, I was taken back to my room where the respiratory technician stayed to connect me back to the ventilator and complete further testing with my breathing. He was slowly weaning me off of the ventilator to see if I was able to breathe on my own. I was. I then was slowly unsedated until I was completely awake, ventilator and feeding tube still in. In order to remove the ventilator, the respiratory technician had to have an order from the ICU doctors though.

Being awake with a ventilator had my blood pressure and heart rate rise off the charts. I was super anxious. But I was awake and alive. I remember how hard it was to sit there and wait for the doctors to do their rounds and make their way to my room. I have a clear memory in my mind. I had a corner room, so I remember seeing the team of doctors all the way down the hallway. Five rooms away. Four rooms away. Three rooms away. Two rooms away. One room away. That last room before mine felt the longest. I probably waited for them for like forty five minutes total, but to me it seemed like five hours because I had a plastic tube shoved down my throat. Worst feeling that I have ever experienced…

The group of ICU doctors finally evaluated me and put in the order to have my ventilator removed. Phewww. Please take this freaking thing out immediately. I then remember staring down the empty hallway from my bed waiting and waiting and waiting for the respiratory technician to come back. "Okay...now!" I would think in my head. But he wouldn't appear. My mom was squeezing my hand on the left side of my bed and my sister, dad, Mike and Brandon took turns coming to my right side to speak to me, even though I wasn't able to respond to them. They weren't sure of the state that I was in but I was all there mentally and I heard and understood every single word that was spoken to me.

After another forty five minutes of waiting, I finally eyed the respiratory technician walking towards my room from down the hallway. I'll never forget what he looked like. He was a Filipino guy, maybe late thirties. He was fairly in shape. I remember that it didn't take long for him to pull the ventilator tube out. It made me gag and cough, but just five seconds, and the thing was out. I hadn't heard myself cough for weeks so I couldn't complain about that. The real test for me was my voice. Was it back? Will I ever be able to talk again?

My family crowded around my bed and my sister, crying, grabbed my hand and said, "I love you." I muttered the words back, "Love you too." Holy shit. My voice was BACK, even though it didn't sound remotely similar to my old voice. It was hoarse and very weak but hearing my voice speak and understand her just made her and everyone around me cry, including my nurse. Looking back, I see how scary of a time that must have been for everyone else around me. For me, I don't think in the moment that I understood just how serious everything was. To be in my state, you must think, of course she knew how serious it was. She wasn't doing anything on her own but breathing. But since I was completely aware for the most part cognitively, I think my brain tricked itself or something into thinking that I wasn't as bad as I actually was. To wake up from a surgery like that, for the third time, in such a risky location, was a miracle in itself.

The fact that I was talking, awake and breathing on my own just one day post-surgery was even more amazing. They were expecting me to be in a coma for some time, potentially forever. I knew that I wasn't ready for heaven yet though and I think the angels that were protecting me knew that also. It was a miracle, and I owed that to the man who saved my life, Dr. Brady. God blessed him and his hands to do miracle work and save lives. We were told that he had done thousands of surgeries, but he never had a patient that had three surgeries, until me.

Dr. Brady and Eliza were still stopping by continuously to check in on me, but this time, I was finally awake with no breathing tube in. I remember seeing them come into my room smiling from ear to ear. I can't even imagine the stress and pressure Dr. Brady must have felt, and then the sense of relief that he felt when he saw me awake with my cognition intact. He came to my bedside and said, "It's gone. It's all out. You had the clearest MRI that we've ever seen from you. I am so happy for you. You've been to the abyss and back, Rachel. You're going to be a grandmother one day." I didn't know what to say to him. My voice was very weak and hoarse from the ventilator, but I looked up at him and the only thing that I could say to him was,

"You saved my life." I just remember looking up at him with no other words.

"No, I don't save lives, God saves lives. We just show up." He said.

"I caught the Hail Mary," I said to him. (He earlier mentioned how my third surgery was the last chance to save me and referenced a "Hail Mary", and I, of course, had to make a football joke about it, in true Rach fashion). Leave it to me to crack a joke after waking up from a coma and intense surgery LOL.

Everyone was laughing. So relieved. And to top it all off, it was New Year's Eve. How ironic? A chance to look forward to healing in the new year, and leave the bad in 2019, not ever looking back at it. I had a lot of work to do. Although I was talking, I still couldn't move my right arm or leg, I had facial paralysis on my left side, my jaw didn't open very wide, I had no hearing in my left ear, I couldn't use the bathroom on my own yet and I had nystagmus in my eyes, meaning that my eyeballs went a little crazy.

The nystagmus wasn't as bad as it had been after the first surgery though, thank God. Instead of my eyeballs spinning around like a windmill, they were jumping up and down like a bouncing basketball. Still not fun, but at least I could open my eyes without feeling like I was going to throw up this time.

Shortly after I woke up, my ICU nurse gave me a breathing treatment. She didn't explain what it was for, but I just assumed that it was to enhance my breathing or something since I just had the tube removed.

She suggested that my family leave the room because she wanted to make sure that I breathed it all in without distraction. All I remember after that was being extremely loopy and kind of dozing off in bed. I felt her rub on my arm to comfort me. I didn't know what she had given me, but I convinced myself that she had drugged me LOL. Why else was my family not allowed to stay in the room with me? It sounds nuts but I was sooo convinced and afraid of her. I was so drugged up though that I couldn't even lift a finger. To me, it was straight out of a horror movie. When my family came back in the room, I whispered to them that the nurse drugged me and I needed a new nurse. Apparently, what she gave me was some kind of pain medication, so I must have just been loopy AF from that. They all just laughed at me.

That night and the next few nights in the intensive care unit, I was still so confused especially when I fell asleep each night. I thought that the bed that I was sleeping in was one of those fake car chairs that they had in barber shops for kids. At night, I thought that I was sleeping in one of those cars, in the front seat of a pick-up truck that had no roof on it- that's what I thought my bed was...?

I still had a feeding tube in my nose, so in order for it to get removed, a speech therapist had to evaluate me eating different things like pudding and graham crackers and watch me drink water before declaring that the tube could be removed. It was such a weird feeling having the feeding tube in- it went up my nose and down my throat into my stomach. I remember whenever they gave me "liquid nutrition", I would feel my nurse inject cold liquid in the tube sticking out of my nose. I would then feel the cold liquid move up my nose, down my throat, down to my stomach and then I felt the cold feeling disappear when it reached my stomach, meaning it had emptied out. That definitely didn't satisfy me like a greasy cheeseburger could.

I was so nervous for the test that would allow them to put the order in to remove my feeding tube. I needed to make sure that I was confident in everything that she was giving me, but the reality was that I didn't know if I was actually able to swallow everything or not. I hadn't been able to eat anything on my own in a long time. As she gave me each item, I took my time, but I was able to do it for the most part. I really wanted to get the tube out because it made me so uncomfortable. I was so excited to be doing so well because I thought that meant that the feeding tube was coming out shortly.

As expected, the speech therapist cleared me to eat, BUT before the feeding tube was to be removed, the doctors wanted me to have one full meal to make sure that I could get the meal down. For my first meal, I wanted to get one of the meals that I had been dreaming about when I couldn't eat at all- chicken nuggets, fries and a frosty from Wendy's. I don't know what had gotten into me- I normally eat pretty healthy, but I had such unhealthy and weird cravings- a burger from Five Guys, a pork roll egg and cheese sandwich, sushi, a bagel from my favorite bagel store. It must have been all of the steroids going to my head...no pun intended there.

My dad went out to get my meal, and returned back with it to my room. Trying to swallow a full meal with a small tube in your throat was pretty challenging. My mom cut the chicken nuggets up into tiny pieces to make it a little easier for me. I honestly didn't trust myself and was afraid that I was going to choke on them. I took a small piece of nugget, and was able to get it down very slowly followed by a fry and a bit of some frosty. Little by little. That's all it would take. And after some time, I did it!!! The nurse was now able to remove my feeding tube. It didn't take long at all for it to come out, but it made me gag because it was pulled out literally from my esophagus. Another step done.

The next morning, my mom noticed my left eye. It was extremely red and irritated. She had my nurse call in an opthamologist consultation, and a few hours later, well into the evening, he showed up. He did a thorough evaluation of my eyes, putting different eye drops in and shining a blue light in my eyes. He discovered that my left eye had developed a huge ulcer in it. It was as big as a dime.

He explained to us that since I had facial paralysis on my left side, it had also affected my eye, which now produced no tears and wasn't able to shut on its own. I also had no feeling in it. Recipe for freaking disaster. I was also super tired and slept a lot during the day, so no one really noticed that my eye was red.

Since it was the end of the day, the eye doctor put a lubricating contact in my eye for protection, and wanted to see how my eye would respond to it overnight. When he returned back the next day, to his surprise, he said that it looked 90% better just from the lubrication. He decided to try it again for a second night, but this time, it didn't work as well. It also didn't stay in place for the whole night. He decided that it would be best to consult a plastic surgeon to stitch my eyelid closed. This would leave a small opening in my eye but it would protect the eye since it didn't close on its own. We also had to put lubricant gel in my eye every few hours to replace its natural tears. He warned us that the plastic surgery team normally took a few days to actually come in. In the meantime, we were told to constantly just lubricate my eye.

After about a week of being in the ICU, I was moved upstairs to the neurology floor again to one of the private rooms. The goal of the private room was to let me get a lot of rest as I was recovering from this major procedure. Unfortunately, that wasn't the case though because I had a very confused and irate neighbor. Her daughter's name was Cheryl, and Cheryl had just left for the night.

My confused neighbor screamed from 5:00 PM that night until 1:00 AM the next morning, then took a few hours off to sleep, then began screaming again at 6:00 AM. "CHERRYYLLL!!! CHHEERRYYYLLL!!! OH CHERYL, YOU'RE NOT COMING BACK FOR ME, ARE YOU!?? CHERYL!!!! PLEASE! PLEASE COME BACK FOR YOUR MAMA!" She was screaming that over and over again while crying. I honestly felt bad for her; it was sad to hear it. She was so confused and angry. My mom went into her room to talk to her at like 6:00 AM that morning to try to calm her down and talk to her.

"What's going on? Whose Cheryl?" My mom asked her.

"My daughter!!!" she wailed.

"Cheryl will be back for you. She just went home for the night to get some sleep but shhh, my baby is sleeping next door."

The woman sat up in her bed and looked at my mom asking, "You got a baby?"

"Yes but shhh, she is sleeping next door."

The woman then goes, "Oh, I'm sorry."

My mom came back to my room, happy that she accomplished her mission of calming my rowdy neighbor down and stopping her from yelling. Five minutes later, we heard her start screaming from next door, "CHERRRYYLL!" Welp. That didn't last very long.

CHAPTER 20

Every morning between 6:30 and 7:00 AM, the neurosurgery residents made rounds on all of the neurosurgery patients. They would come into my room every morning when I was either sleeping or dozing off again from my night of sleep. They would flip the lights on to make my room super bright. There were about three of them each time and they would perform neurological tests on me that required me to use my brain...it didn't work well that early in the morning, especially after the shape it was in. "Follow my finger with your eyes...squeeze my hands... push down on my hand with your foot like you're hitting the gas pedal. Can you move your right arm at all for us?"

They knew that I lost all movement of my right side but they wanted to see if I was able to do anything as a baseline. I tried with every ounce of my being to move my arm, but trying to move it felt like I was lifting a 1,000 pound boulder. It was damn near impossible. "Wait, do that again!" One of the residents shouted. I tried with all of my might to lift it again, and this time I looked down to see that my shoulder moved ever so slightly. "Rachel, that's amazing! You're only a week out of your surgery!"

Twenty minutes later, six more residents showed up to my room, crowding around my bed. "Can you show everyone else what you were able to do for us a couple of minutes ago?" I tried to move my arm, and saw my right shoulder raise up a little again. It felt like I was using all of the power that my body was able to exert. "Wow, Rachel, that's so amazing!!!" another resident said. The rest of them commented on my newly acquired skill, before leaving to finish with the rest of their rounds.

Time went so slowly when I laid in a hospital bed each day, staring at the wall in front of me because I couldn't hear or see the TV and couldn't see my phone, so all I did was just lay there and think about the pain that I was in. On one of the hospital TV stations, they had a pre-recorded session of a woman doing a guided meditation that was for healing and relaxation. My mom played it for me often and I'd have the remote control with the television speaker resting next to my ear on full blast and listen with my eyes closed. That's the only way I could hear anything. I'd listen to every single one of her words and relax my body. I tried to believe that as she spoke about healing my pain, it would actually heal my pain.

Mom also found a channel on TV that was playing my favorite movie ever, Elf. I couldn't see but I could listen. I basically memorized that movie line by line, so although I couldn't watch, I visualized the scenes as I heard them through the speaker and was cracking up. Will Ferrell is the best- that movie always got me.

In the afternoon that day, Dr. Brady came to check in on me. A lot of the time, he would be talking to my family because I was so slow to respond and really couldn't hear anything that well. I would just look at him, nod my head and smile pretending that I heard him even though I couldn't hear shit, LOL. He explained to my family that he was extremely concerned about my weight.

I was told that I must have lost between 40-50 pounds. I weigh about 135 when I'm healthy, to put things into perspective. It wasn't a surprise to anyone that I had lost so much weight because I wasn't eating for days before they even put my feeding tube in. Even then, once the feeding tube was in, it was just giving me the bare minimum of what my body needed to fuel itself.

My family was told by Dr. Brady to give me calories, calories, calories. That's when the meal replacement supplement drinks started up between meals. I'd get one Ensure as soon as I woke up before breakfast, eat breakfast, have another Ensure, have lunch, have a milkshake, eat dinner. Now that I could eat again, it was no problem for me to take in the extra calories- especially being on those steroids again. The chocolate Ensure flavor grew on me too- it really wasn't bad.

While in bed one day, I started feeling heart palpitations occur randomly so my nurse put stickers on my chest and clipped wires to the stickers to monitor my heart rate from the nurses station. As I would just be laying in bed, not moving a muscle, nurses would randomly come running into my room. "What happened?! Are you okay? Your heart rate is at 170 right now!"

My body was literally messing with me. Part of the brain stem controlled heart rate, and since my brain stem was disrupted multiple times, my heart rate went crazy even when I was doing absolutely nothing but resting. While just laying in bed, it kept jumping off the charts randomly. Another reason why my heart rate went berserk though was when the physical therapists came to my room to try and get me out of my bed. The high heart rate wasn't a coincidence, though. I couldn't do much so they'd basically just be lifting me up and plopping me down on the chair. I was really nervous to even have them touch me. Just by seeing them enter my room, the fear and anxiety in me would make my heart rate spike up.

I kept thinking about the occupational therapist before this last surgery that "tossed me around like a rag doll". I was sooo scared from that experience because of how weak my body was. My heart rate would be so high that these therapists weren't allowed to do anything with me for safety reasons. The one time that they distracted me by asking me random questions, they got my heart rate within normal range. They were able to transfer me into the chair. I had to stand up, turn around, and sit down behind me. That's it. I had to be assisted by like three therapists to even sit up in bed and when I stood on my two feet for the first time, it was a feeling unlike any other. I'll never forget it- I could only feel my left leg supporting me.

It felt as if my right leg was amputated or just disappeared. Even though both legs were there, I could only put my body weight through my left leg. It really felt like the right leg wasn't there at all. I had no center of gravity either. As soon as I was standing, my body toppled over to the side. Luckily, a therapist was there to catch me before I completely fell over. My torso was weaker than a wet napkin.

As soon as they got me into the chair, all I wanted to do was go back to the bed. It was so uncomfortable for me and used so much effort in my muscles to sit upright when all that my body wanted to do was just slouch over. The therapists had to see me sitting in a chair at least one time before they were able to write a script for my discharge to go to rehab. Everyone believed that getting me up and moving would circulate the blood to my brain and be beneficial for me. It would help me start my recovery but I was so tired that I couldn't even keep my eyes open for more than an hour at a time.

We now had the discharge note from the hospital's physical therapy team, but before I could be transferred to rehab, we had to wait for the plastic surgery team to see me to stitch my eyelid closed. My nurse called the plastic's team to get an ETA of when they would be arriving. They informed her that it would be the next day.

That night, two of the techs on the floor that were close to my age were in the room to clean me up but also to just hangout with me. They stayed in the room for a while afterwards talking to me; it was really nice. I grew close to a lot of the techs and nurses on that floor because I was in and out of the hospital so many times but also because a lot of them were close to my age.

One of them brought a body wash in from home just for me so that I wouldn't have to use the boring one that was provided by the hospital. It was such a sweet and thoughtful gesture for her to do. After they were done cleaning me up, they had to turn me onto my side to assist me with putting a hospital gown back on. When I turned onto my right side, I felt alright. When I turned on my left side, I felt horrible. Crazy vertigo, my eyes actually blacked out, my head pounded.

Every morning when I woke up, I still had the jumping nystagmus in my eyes that I was really hoping would go away. I kept reverting back to my first surgery and remembered that it went away within a few days. "If only my nystagmus went away, everything would feel so much better," I would think.

I couldn't understand why it wasn't going away as fast as it did the first time- it was debilitating to me and made me feel so horrible. In the early afternoon, the plastic surgery team arrived at my room. There were two women in their early thirties and a man in his sixties. My anxiety was bad knowing that they were there to put a stitch on my eyelid. It made things worse when they asked my mom and dad to exit the room for the procedure. They put my hospital bed all the way back so that it was flat. One of the girls shined a light on my eye. The other girl grabbed my hand because she knew I was probably freaking out- who wouldn't?!? I just closed my eyes the whole time. The doctor injected a numbing agent on my eyelid. I just remember feeling a lot of tugging and pulling on my eye but that was it- no pain.

The procedure took only twenty five minutes; it wasn't bad! My nurse set up a discharge for me and set up my transportation to go to rehab the following day. I was low key pretty happy to hear that I had one last day at the hospital before going back to rehab because I was so afraid of getting thrown around again. The thought of having therapy really terrified me.

The day of my transfer back to rehab was January 8, 2020. I was taken in the morning via ambulance to begin my recovery. I was completely bundled up in my stretcher with hospital blankets and a fuzzy pink jacket that a friend gifted me. It was a blustery cold January day in New Jersey. I was so comfortable and warm until about halfway through the ambulance ride where I thought I was going to pass out from heat exhaustion. I guess the combo of the heat in the ambulance and being bundled up was too much for me and I was dripping sweat. Trying to remove my jacket was a rude awakening for what I was in for when dressing and undressing myself. Removing my jacket with one arm seemed like one of the most difficult tasks and it was making me sweat even more.

When I arrived at rehab, they actually put me back in the same exact room that I was in the first time. The first thing that they did was transfer me from the ambulance stretcher to the hospital bed. A male tech helped the ambulance crew shimmy me over from the stretcher to the bed. It always scared me when they did this- they lifted the sheets under me from the stretcher and used that to basically lift me onto the bed- it also really just hurt my head having any movement.

I was so amazed because during my first stay, I remembered hearing that tech's voice, but I could never actually look at him and see what he looked like. I also remember the room being a little bit different then how I remembered it from my first stay there. I still couldn't turn my head to look out the window yet, but I just pictured the room looking a lot bigger than it actually was. I was honestly in my own little world the last time I was in this room.

My family followed in their cars behind the ambulance, so they were right there with me too when I arrived. I knew that this time post-surgery, it was different. I still had pain in my head, but the pain felt different. It didn't feel like extreme pressure pain anymore. After the first and second surgery, it felt like my brain was swelling in my skull, but the skull restricted my brain from expanding. This time, it was still painful, but a different kind of pain.

I had a rehab doctor who would see me just about every-day- his name was Dr. Cohen. He was my doctor the last time that I was at rehab too. I remember seeing his green New York Jets lanyard but I wasn't able to see his face. This time, I saw his lanyard and was able to see his face too. My therapy began on Thursday, January 9, 2020. I had an hour of speech therapy, followed by an hour of physical therapy, followed by an hour of occupational therapy. My speech therapist was not the same every day, but my other therapists were consistently working with me.

The second day of therapy, my physical therapist tried getting me to walk for the first time. I wouldn't call it much of a walk though. It was more like a carry by my therapist. It looked like I was an infant being forced to walk but it was too early in life to do so, LOL. I look back at the recording that was taken of me during this walk and I can see just how weak my entire body was-Literally every muscle. I didn't feel that my right leg was actually there to support me because all of the weight was taken in my left leg.

I took maybe four steps, legit being dragged before plopping back down into the wheelchair behind me. They had to give me a special wheelchair too that was tall in the back to support my neck because I was too weak to hold my head up. On the evening of my third day at rehab, I started feeling feverish. The material of my t-shirt rubbing against my skin was hurting, and I felt achy and hot. I called my nurse in my room to take my temperature. Low and behold, my temperature was 102. "You're joking. Why me? What did I do to deserve this?" I thought.

The nurse gave me Tylenol to take the fever away and I fell asleep. By 8:30 PM on most days I was struggling to stay awake anyway. By 11:30 PM that night, I woke up because I was so uncomfortable. The nurse checked my temperature again and this time it went up to 103. I thought that Tylenol was going to stop my fever, but a few hours after taking it, my fever was even higher. Also, the nystagmus in my eyes got even more intense because of my elevated body temperature.

Though it was the middle of the night, we wanted the on-call doctor to assess me to make sure that it wasn't a complication from my brain again. By the time that the doctor arrived in my room, it was 3:00 AM. I had gotten a second round of Tylenol, but the fever still stayed the exact same at 103. This doctor was more of a general internist, not a neurologist, so it was kind of obvious that she didn't know how to answer questions pertaining to my brain. Of course, this was also late on Friday night into early Saturday morning, so Dr. Cohen wouldn't be back in the hospital until Monday.

The on-call doctor said that she was going to order blood work and a CT scan to see if she could find the reason for my fever. I was able to go back to bed for a few hours but woke up burning up again. The nurse took my temperature and it was at 102. I took some more Tylenol, but it did nothing to break the fever. My blood was drawn and I was taken down for a cat scan, but the results showed no evidence of an infection or anything concerning.

In rehab, I had five weekdays of therapy, but on the first weekend there, I had therapy. After the first weekend, I was put on the off day schedule randomly if I was lucky. Of course, my first weekend there was when I had 102 fever days and 103 fever nights. The therapist for physical therapy stopped by my room to pick me up and bring me to the gym. "Are you ready to get to work?" He asked me, enthusiastically. The last thing that I wanted to do was workout, but my mom nailed in my head that if I declined doing any therapy, my insurance would stop covering my stay, forcing me to go home.

"Is there any way we can just do some workouts from my bed?" I asked politely. "I'm not feeling well today."

"Sure, that's not a problem. Let me just grab some equipment from the gym and I'll be right back."

Low and behold, there I was laying in my bed, with 102 fever, doing freaking leg lifts. I cannot make this shit up if I tried. For the next three days, my fever was at 102 during the day, and 103 at night. The fever never broke once. The doctors and nurses tested me for the flu, pricked me and poked me, gave me X-rays, and other tests, but still couldn't find the source of my fever. The gray area girl was at it again…

CHAPTER 21

Since one of the many things that the brain stem controlled was body temperature, Dr. Cohen came to the conclusion that my body temperature was out of whack and trying to level itself out again after my surgery. This sounds disgusting, but because I had a brain surgery in the beginning of December and then a second one at the end of December, I wasn't allowed to wash my hair basically for the whole month.

I was dying to wash my hair for weeks and Dr. Cohen knew that. He was in touch with Dr. Brady about me constantly and finally got the OK from him to let me wash my hair. The only restriction was that I had to use a mild baby shampoo and no conditioner. I didn't care, I'd do just about anything to wash my hair. You take what you can get. A tech and my mom wheeled me down the hallway and into the shower room to assist me. Since I couldn't stand up, I was wheeled into the shower stall with my big ass wheelchair. It was able to recline so the tech was able to wash my hair without getting the rest of my body wet. It felt amazing. I can't even describe how it felt to wash my hair after a freaking month.

After cleaning my hair, my mom showed me the huge wad of hair that was on the floor- it was what fell out of my head. We just giggled about it though. My girls and long haired fellas reading this, you know that in almost every shower that you take, it seems like a ton of hair falls out. Imagine a month-long build up of loose hair, just waiting to fall out when you showered- yeah, that was what was on the floor near the drain.

That night as I was going to bed, I noticed that my stitched eye was open...unstitched. The temporary stitch must have popped open at some point. I let my nurse know, who said that she was going to consult an eye doctor the following morning. I was nervous the whole night about my eye though- I was afraid that it would dry out and develop another ulcer from being open.

The following day, an eye doctor came somewhat early, prepared to stitch up my eye for the second time. He performed the procedure from my room, and it took approximately twenty minutes. I was pretty proud of myself because I didn't require taking any Xanax to get myself through it. The next time that I washed my hair, another huge wad of hair fell out. Then the next time, another huge wad. OK, this wasn't normal anymore. Chunks of my scalp started to show from bald spots that developed and the hair in my ponytail was getting thinner and thinner by the day.

Every time I laid back on my pillow after taking a shower, a ton of loose hair would be on my pillow- my hair was falling out. A lot. We never got a real answer as to why the heck this was happening to me. We speculated that it was from all of the radiation that I was exposed to over the past couple of months, or maybe from medication, or maybe from the extreme stress that my body had been put through. I guess we'll never really know the true answer- all I know is that I basically had no hair left. As if all of the other deficits weren't enough to deal with, now I was losing all of my hair too.

I also developed daily nosebleeds from my left nostril. The dry air made my nose develop an ulcer, which was the source of the bleeding. We only discovered that after I had my nostril cauterized by an ENT in rehab.

I remember waking up every morning, opening my eyes and hoping for no nystagmus. I didn't understand why it was taking so long to go away. On a number of mornings, it was so debilitating that I felt like the whole room was shaking.

My sister was so amazing to me while I was in rehab. She would arrive early every morning to sit with my mom and I before reporting into work. She would come upstairs to eat her lunch with me every day, come in on her day off to spend the day with me and come a lot of the time on the weekend to see me. Brandon came whenever he could. He worked late hours almost every day, but would always stop by after work, whether he just came in for ten minutes to give me a kiss goodnight or stayed for an hour to hang out with me before I went to sleep.

My dad and Mike came everyday too, even if I was napping or in therapy, they'd be there. My mom takes the cake though for being with me. Since my surgeries, she hadn't left my side. She would sleep over with me on the recliner chair every night- I honestly don't know what I would do without her. She was my advocate for everything, and helped me do basically everything. I never thought I would spend that much time with her, but I am so grateful for her.

Getting used to the feeling of my new body when half of it was numb was a really big adjustment for me. I would sit on my hand and not even know it unless someone told me. When I sat down, my leg would shoot straight out and kick things- I didn't feel it but it definitely wouldn't feel good if I could.

My occupational therapist was amazing. When I first started working with her, I couldn't sit at the edge of my bed without falling over to one side. She would have me stand on my knees and lean against a bolster sometimes, but it felt almost impossible to pull myself up and keep myself up. My core strength was equivalent to jello. We worked on a ton of core, arm strengthening and coordination exercises. We even worked on life skills like dressing myself and getting in and out of the shower. She would pull me to do more therapy even when she was done working for the day. She knew that I wouldn't say no to doing anything. She also bought me some things that I could use to work on my arm with her own money. It was so obvious that she cared so deeply about me and my recovery.

My physical therapist was beyond amazing also. She worked me hard but it's because she wanted me to get better. I remember the first time that she had me try to get off of the floor, it was impossible. I literally fell flat on my face at one point. We worked with every walking device and contraption that you could think of. She even had me in a harness at one point, walking around the hallways as the nurses cheered me on. I really connected with her, not only as my therapist, but as my friend. She was Polish, so she cooked me homemade pierogies when I got sick of eating hospital food. Let me just say, they were amazing!

I don't remember how or when I first noticed it, but my eye stitch popped open again! This would be the third time! This time, they decided to call in an ocular plastic surgeon to put my stitches in. I remember the evening that he came to do the procedure, my mom, dad, Rebecca and Brandon were there. My dad had just picked up a pizza for us all to eat. Just as I was about to be wheeled to the rec room to eat, the plastic surgeon arrived at my room. Honestly, by the third time I was stitched, I had gotten used to it and I was totally fine, actually unphased. I just wanted it to be over with so that I could go eat some freaking pizza.

One of my rehab nurses, Joanna, was so sweet and awesome. She wanted to keep me entertained during my days in rehab and knew that I loved art and DIY things. The Giants had sent me a big, beautiful arrangement of roses that were on my windowsill, but starting to wither a bit. Joanna sat with me after her shift one day and made a wreath out of those beautiful flowers! Another day, Joanna brought in her watercolor set- paint, brushes and paper. Her goal was to find me a new hobby that I was able to do and enjoy. I must say, the watercolor painting was a great idea that really stuck. Although I had to do it left-handed, watercolors were so forgiving and fun to do. I really appreciated her thoughtfulness.

I watched Super Bowl Sunday lying in the hospital bed next to Brandon. I couldn't really see what was happening because of my crazy jumping eyes so I basically had to ask him what was happening the whole time. To be honest, I couldn't even tell you who was in that Super Bowl- Kansas City aaaand?? I couldn't make it past halftime either. I was so exhausted. Isn't it ironic that a year or two earlier, I traveled to and worked at the Super Bowl and now I was in a hospital bed watching it, unable to even know what the heck was going on? Before the game, Brandon signed me out at the nurses station to take me downstairs to the lobby. They had a big fish tank there and we would just sit in front of it and watch the fish swim around. It didn't take much to entertain me these days.

I had something called drop foot on my right foot, which basically happened after my stroke. I wasn't able to lift my toes up, so it made me drag my foot. My physical therapist wrapped my foot up with an ace bandage everyday, in the interim, until I could be fitted for a custom AFO brace by a man named Ben. I remember when he molded my foot for the brace. He was talking to me, but I could barely hear a word that he was saying. I was able to make out that he was asking me about football at one point, but I don't even remember if or how I responded to him. My other therapists knew that I had trouble hearing, so they'd basically be screaming in my ear for me to hear.

After Ben left that day, my therapist told me a story about him. When he was in his twenties, he had some kind of infection that paralyzed him from the neck down. It took him a long time to recover, but he did it. And now you couldn't tell that anything like that ever happened to him. I know that our situations are totally different, but similar in the sense that something horrible happened to us in our twenties, and we're both driven to do good. But his drive helped him get better. His story really moved me and gave me a lot of motivation.

When he brought my custom AFO brace in, it was almost like night and day for my walking pattern. I was still nowhere close to having my balance yet, but the brace that he made prevented my knee from snapping, prevented my ankle from rolling, and stopped my drop foot from dragging on the floor. I didn't know how much I needed that brace until I had it on me. My therapist and I were experimenting with different devices to walk with, and ultimately decided that a hemi walker would be the safest device for me to start with. I wasn't able to walk alone yet, and basically had to be carried across the gym to keep myself upright, but we thought that a hemi walker worked best for me to go home with safely.

Since I had paralysis on the left side of my face and the right side of my body, feeding myself was like a toddler that was introduced to a utensil for the first time. I had to wear a towel as a bib, and would be lucky if one out of every ten bites actually made it into my mouth, instead of in my lap. The paralysis stopped me from opening part of my mouth, so the food would bounce off of my lip and fall off of my fork. It also didn't help that I was a righty trying to feed myself with my left hand now.

I was also on steroids again, so my appetite was wild. My breakfast would start out with the meal that I ordered (usually pancakes or scrambled eggs). I would then eat a whole bowl of oatmeal, a bowl of cereal, and a fruit cup. Oh, and an Ensure of course. These steroids were no joke!!! I was starting to learn that foods that I was able to pick up with my hand were still a mess, but a little more tolerable to eat. Since I couldn't feel my lip, tongue or cheek on the left side, I would constantly bite it and make myself bleed. I also would get severe acid reflux when I ate.

One afternoon, I ordered a chicken quesadilla for lunch. It came with sour cream on the side. My mom, Mike and Rebecca were in my room with me at the time when it was delivered. I had my towel bib on, ready to roll. I started eating and everyone went about their business, speaking about who knows what. I wasn't even paying attention. I dipped my quesadilla in the sour cream and took a huge bite. I felt the sour cream go all over my cheek but figured that they all weren't paying attention anyway so I just said F it. I picked up my quesadilla and used it as a napkin to wipe the sour cream off of my face- I figured that it'd be a shame to waste it on a napkin, right? Just as I wiped the quesadilla across my face, Mike and I made eye contact. "Shit, he saw me!" I thought. "I saw that, Rachel," he said and started cracking up. We still laugh about that to this day.

Insurance was starting to give me issues about covering my stay at rehab, and they wanted to send me home. I was nowhere near ready to go home though. I couldn't even walk alone yet, I couldn't transfer from my bed to the bedside commode, I could barely even hold myself up if I wasn't leaning against the back of my bed. Dr. Cohen and my therapists came to an agreement with my insurance company on a discharge date.

The day before I was supposed to be sent home, Dr. Cohen came into the gym to watch me walk. He said that after watching me that day, he had concerns about sending me home. He felt unsure if it would be a safe discharge. He spoke with my insurance company and was able to get me an extension of only a few days, but not much. I had many, many MRI's of my brain over the last couple of months, but I had my last and final one as an inpatient on February 20, 2020, mom's birthday. It was an incredible feeling knowing that it was my last one, for now.

CHAPTER 22

I left inpatient rehab on February 22, 2020. I couldn't believe that I would finally be home- it felt like it was too good to be true. So many nights in the hospital, I dreamed about the day that I would be sleeping in the coziness of my own bed again. I just couldn't believe that it was actually happening.

I was wheeled down to the car by one of my nurses. It was my first time being in an actual car in months. As we were driving out of the town where my rehab hospital was, my mom showed me all of the different places where everyone that had visited me had gone out for food. I tried to focus my eyes to see where she was pointing to but my eyes wouldn't let me. It was weird because I stayed at that hospital for weeks and weeks, but the town outside of the hospital walls was completely foreign to me. It felt like it was my first time there.

After a few days of being home, I was finally settling in. However, I was starting to realize just how difficult it was to do simple tasks now like putting on a t-shirt without hitting me eye. I only had one arm to use and I couldn't stand up. Changing clothes, brushing my teeth, washing my hands. Almost impossible for me as I tried to navigate life with my new body. Taking the garbage out, doing laundry that was down a flight of 12 stairs, showering while standing up? Actually impossible.

During my first shower at home, I had to put a towel down on my plastic shower chair because I wasn't strong enough to hold myself up and not slide off of the chair. I had to wear water shoes too so my feet wouldn't slip either. As I was trying to get the t-shirt over my head while getting dressed, I hit my face with my shirt and popped the stitch on my eyelid open AGAIN!!! It felt like someone was playing a sick joke on me that this was happening for a fourth time.

We called the ocular plastic surgeon that I had seen in the hospital. He instructed us to come to his office. My mom drove me there and my dad met us there to help with my wheelchair and get me in and out of the car. Since this was the fourth time that my eye would be stitched now, he recommended a tarsorrhaphy. This was a procedure where he would permanently fuse my top eyelid to my bottom eyelid. This would make sure that the stitches would not open anymore. He also predicted that my eyelid wouldn't be able to shut on its own for a while, so this was more of a long term solution. Of course, I would be able to reverse this down the road by having my eyelid cut open again.

I decided to move forward with the more permanent procedure, which took about an hour to complete. It was night time by the time that we left his office- no one was there anymore but us. I remember getting into the passenger seat of the car afterwards. I pulled down the mirror to see what I looked like and started crying immediately. I looked like a monster- who was that person that was in the reflection? It wasn't the girl that I once knew. I cried the whole ride home, no exaggeration.

Trying to transition at home was so difficult at first, especially because I still required so much care. Brandon worked late basically everyday, so my mom, dad, and sister came over in shifts to assist me. There was a night when my mom was cooking dinner and I was sitting at the kitchen table. Mike and Brandon were there too, just hanging out on the couch. I wasn't sitting on the dining room chair for long before my body crumbled on me like quick sand. I couldn't hold myself up while sitting there anymore and toppled to my right side out of the chair and onto the floor.

On one of the next few days, I restarted at outpatient therapy again. I had the same two physical therapists as I did the first time that I was there, a new occupational therapist, and now was beginning speech therapy too. I was so not myself in therapy. The best way to describe me was fog brained. I was basically just "there" physically. My eyes had no life in them and my bubbly personality was empty. I wore a baseball cap to hide my "hair" or lack of it. On my first week back at therapy, my physical therapist made a joke to me, "Wow, one of my patients canceled their appointment this afternoon because they are scared of the Coronavirus. Isn't that so ridiculous and dumb?" He said, laughing.

Prior to that mention of the Coronavirus, I heard little rumblings about it on the news, but I just put it in one ear and out the other. Things like the Swine flu were things that you heard about but then forgot about quickly. I was thinking it was going to be something like that. As the week went on, the news stations started to talk about this new virus more and more. They talked about how it was starting to enter the USA and spread pretty rapidly.

I remember being in therapy that day after watching the news and I had to sneeze really bad. I was trying with every ounce of my body to stop the sneeze from coming out though so that people wouldn't stare at me and think that I was sick. I could tell that people were starting to become paranoid, especially at therapy, where there were a lot of older people. After therapy that day, I went to Walmart with my mom. It was my first real outing since I got out of the hospital. I was in one of those electric carts that rode around the store. I remember my Nanny always needed one to get around stores when she shopped, but I never imagined that I, at twenty five years old, would be using one too. I just tried to ignore the fact that I knew people would be staring at me.

My mom had some items on her list that she needed to shop for, and I had one thing that I specifically needed. I wanted to get a foaming hand sanitizer because washing my hands was very difficult now, and I used foaming sanitizer all the time in the hospital to make my life easier. It covered more surface area to spread around on my hands since it was foam.

We couldn't find it anywhere though so we decided to ask an employee who was passing by where we'd be able to find it. "Haha, we ran out of all of our hand sanitizer days ago," she laughed.

As we scanned the next aisle, we noticed that the whole toilet paper section was empty. Literally, every brand...gone. WTF? "Well, that's stupid," I thought. It felt like a New Jersey state of emergency for a snowstorm. People would panic and buy all of the canned goods, milk, and bread that they could get their hands on just because. That's what I thought about this virus. I thought that it was dumb in the first place that people were buying all of the hand sanitizer in the store, but I understood that the sanitizer was a quick way to get rid of germs. But toilet paper? Why the heck would people hoard that? Did they think that this was an apocalypse or something? And even then, wouldn't you rather have extra food than extra toilet paper??

Anyway, we continued on with our shopping. I couldn't see shit and driving an electric cart probably wasn't the smartest idea because of that. I was also terrified to fall out of the seat since I fell out of my chair a few days earlier. When I turned the next corner, I thought I had more room but I misjudged it and rammed into a refrigerator filled with cans of whipped cream. Oopsie. I guess that's why I'm not allowed to drive a real car. That was nothing compared to what I did down the next aisle. Not only did I hit the end cap filled with pasta, but I slammed into it so hard that I actually got the shelf stuck under my cart. My mom had to lift the shelf up to free it from my cart. Pasta boxes were scattered all over the floor that my mom quickly picked up trying not to make a scene. We were both cracking up.

After scanning through a couple more aisles, we turned the corner and I slammed into a cardboard display of Saltine crackers. Luckily, I didn't hit it hard enough to knock the pyramid of crackers down. But that was it- cut me off. It was time for us to go!

CHAPTER 23

On Monday, March 16, 2020, I was scheduled to go to therapy. I was starting to feel uncomfortable though by what the news had been saying all weekend. All that they were talking about was this Coronavirus or "COVID-19" and how dangerous and contagious it was. Apparently, cases were rising in the USA everyday. I was freaked out because I'm a germaphobe as it is, so I pleaded with my mom to let me stay home from therapy at least for a few days until things settled down.

She insisted that I went to therapy at least on Monday though so that my therapists and I could create a plan for me to do at home. My first appointment that day was in speech therapy. I told my therapist about my plans to take the rest of the week off. She called my other two therapists into her office to have a little meeting with me. I had my speech appointment first, and then afterwards my physical therapist and occupational therapist were going to take me to a private room upstairs to go over a couple of exercises to do at home that week. I was uncomfortable to be in a big, open gym with random people because of everything that I'd been hearing on the news.

Since my recovery was so out of the ordinary, my speech therapist sometimes had a second speech therapist watch our sessions to see what kind of things we'd be working on. Halfway through the session that day, the second therapist in the room read us a text message from her daughter. It said something along the lines of 'her daughter's friend's father worked for the office of homeland security, and told her that supermarkets were going to be shut down in twenty four hours, so grab as much food as you can get.'

In the matter of hours, the virus turned from light chatter to extremely serious and scary! Was that true? I didn't know what to believe or who to listen to.

After speech therapy, my other therapists picked me up and brought me upstairs. We went over a few things to work on my arm and some stuff that I could do to work my leg. I was only planning to take the rest of the week off though so we didn't go over too much stuff together. I really wished that they had written things down for me, because almost instantly, I forgot what we went over. My brain wasn't able to obtain and remember a ton of information at once at the time.

After I left therapy that day, I went over what I could remember with my mother, hoping that she would remember more than I would be able to. I was really excited because the next day, Tuesday, March 17, I was supposed to see Dr. Brady for my first post-op follow up. Being reassured by the guy who was actually in my brain was all that I needed at that time to feel okay. I really just wanted to know that I was on track so far.

It was now around 4:00 PM on Monday. I was watching the news again. Shit was getting real serious, and what I was hearing was starting to really scare me. They were saying how severe COVID-19 could get, really quickly. How healthy people were getting sick and ending up on ventilators in ICU's. Was I more at risk because my body had just gone through so much trauma? "You know what, Rachel? I'm almost thinking that we should just pack up a bag for you and go to my house for the week," my mom said.

Brandon was exposed to other people at work all day so we were afraid that if he were to accidentally bring it home, my body would have a really hard time fighting it off. She was right. We didn't know much about the virus at all and what it was capable of doing to my body. We didn't want to take any chances though if it was as contagious and dangerous as people were claiming it was. I'm usually a worry wart and a total hypochondriac, but when my mom started to agree with me, I worried even more.

She called Mike, asking what his opinion was about packing up and going to their house for a few days. They were teetering back and forth, but ultimately decided that I should go. It would be safer for my weak, healing body. Now that a decision was made, I wanted to pack up and be out ASAP. I had so much stuff that needed to come with me. The problem was, I couldn't even stand or see straight to help my mom pack everything. Not only did I have a bag with clothes but I had a wheelchair, hemi-walker, pillows, medicine, and night braces. I watched my mom take a few trips back and forth to her car to load up my stuff. I felt horrible that I had to just sit there and watch.

On her last trip back up the steps, she came to help me out of the house. I obviously couldn't walk on my own yet, so I had to be basically held upright to make it to the car safely. Once we got on the road, I called Brandon to give him a heads up about what was happening. I explained to him that it was the safest place for me to go right now, and he agreed with me and understood. Besides, it was only going to be for a week or two.

While we were still in the car, we got a call from Eliza, Dr. Brady's PA. She was calling us to cancel my appointment for the next day. She told us that because of the coronavirus, he was not going to be seeing any patients unless it was an emergency. She also told us that she thought it would be a good idea to take a few days off from therapy. She said that I should be quarantined somewhere to stay safe because I was in such a fragile state. As literal minutes went by, it was getting more serious.

"Should I be worried though? Am I more at risk?" I asked her.

"Well, you don't have an underlying condition but we don't even want you to get a cold at this point. You can't have any more setbacks."

She was right. They all say in your first six months after brain surgery, you make a lot of recovery. In my first six months after my brain surgery, I had two more brain surgeries. I really couldn't afford to have more setbacks. Just because I wasn't in therapy didn't mean that I wasn't working on my own that week, though. My mom and Mike would take me outside to walk and I would try to work out my arm from the couch. I also tried to do fifty sit-ups a day. That Friday, March 20, 2020, we got a call saying that my therapy facility was shutting down for two weeks because of COVID-19. Wow, for my therapy to be shutting down? What the???

The scariest part of everything happening was that nobody knew much about this virus, or what it was capable of doing. Not even doctors or scientists. Within days, the hospitals in New York and New Jersey were overflowing, their ICUs were overflowing, and there was a shortage of masks and ventilators all over the country. This wasn't just a normal "flu". It seemed like it could affect anyone. Healthy or not, young or old.

The CDC knew early on that kids weren't really affected as seriously, and the most at-risk people were the elderly or those with underlying conditions, but anyone could still get it and anyone could still get really sick from it. They said that people could also contract the virus and be asymptomatic, meaning that they could spread it without even showing symptoms of carrying it.

New York City was the epicenter of new cases, and New Jersey was right behind them. It made sense because a lot of people that live in New Jersey commute into Manhattan for work. Every day, my mom, Mike and I would watch our governor Phil Murphy on TV hold daily press conferences showing us daily increases by the thousands. Thousands of new cases, hospitalizations, ICU admissions, ventilator usage, and deaths.

It really seemed like in one day or in the blink of an eye, it became totally out of control. The scariest part of it all was that even the CDC didn't know how it was contracted, if it stayed live on surfaces, or if it was even safe to be outdoors. The news channels informed us that we should create cloth masks to cover our nose and mouth. Luckily, from all of my prior hospital visits, we had already bought disposable surgical masks to use.

Over the next couple of days, we learned that COVID-19 was contracted by droplets that came from your nose or mouth getting into other people's noses or mouths. We learned that you couldn't wear a mask to prevent yourself from getting it, but you could wear a mask to prevent spreading it. This basically meant that you couldn't be responsible for yourself. You had to rely on others to keep yourself safe. We also learned that it was safe to be outside.

Once we learned that being outside was safe, we really took advantage of that. I had a routine every day- wake up, eat breakfast, do speech exercises, go on a walk outside with my mom and

Mike, do occupational therapy and physical therapy exercises on the couch, complete my sit-ups, do speech exercises again, then chill out until dinner time. The "outdoor walk" consisted of my mom and Mike taking turns pushing me in my wheelchair; then I would get out of the wheelchair, walk ten feet with my hemi walker (being basically dragged) and plopping back into my wheelchair. That was my "walk". I was sooo unstable and weak.

Two weeks after my canceled appointment with Dr. Brady, I had a virtual appointment with him over video chat. Although I was pretty bummed that I couldn't see him in person, it was good to see him at all. New York was getting worse and worse by the day though. They shut down all "elective surgeries" there. They had to send in the S.S. Comfort Navy ship to dock in the New York harbor and house hospital patients because the hospitals were literally overflowing and overwhelmed with patients.

They had to fly in doctors and nurses from different states to aid the doctors and nurses from New York City to tend to all of the patients. New Jersey was not much better. Hospitals were crazy packed here too so they had to transform expo centers into hospital pods to treat patients with just a curtain separating one patient from the next. It was total madness.

The virus seemed to come on so quick that nobody was prepared for it in the slightest; not even our government. Ventilators were needed all over the place and there were not enough available. Hand sanitizer was out of stock everywhere so distilleries were using their alcohol to make hand sanitizer to give out. Clothing stores were cutting "masks" out of cloth fabric and giving them out for free. I have never seen anything like it in my life. It felt like a zombie apocalypse, or as if the world was ending. Everyone was afraid to be out in public or to be around other people.

Companies were shutting down and having their employees work from home unless they were essential workers- grocery store workers that ran the stores, health care workers in hospitals, police officers, and package carriers to deliver medical supplies. Of course, Rebecca was a healthcare worker and Brandon was a package carrier. I was quarantined from them as well as my dad. I received another call from my therapy facility that therapy would be closed "until further notice" now. It really sucked because this was the most crucial time to be in therapy for me, and I really wasn't there for long at all to learn what I could be doing at home.

Mike would wake up early on days that he went out food shopping just as the supermarkets opened for the day. They had a designated time in the morning for 60+ shoppers to get their groceries during that time, so it had less crowds. As soon as he got home with the groceries, my mom would wash every item with soap and water before putting it away, including the fruit and boxed items. We didn't know if the virus stuck to surfaces yet, so we didn't want to take any chances.

But each day, I was starting to feel more and more like myself again, and felt myself getting stronger. I remember when I was still in the hospital, Dr. Brady said that one of the most important things for me to do was to walk, walk, walk, walk, walk. I was very determined to keep my recovery moving forward despite not being able to be in therapy. I didn't necessarily know what kind of exercises I could be doing, but I knew that walking would help me.

Rain or shine, Mike, my mom and I would go on walks. That was our daily routine, and probably what kept us all sane, those daily walks outside. On rainy days, I would go up and down the stairwell, which was four floors, and walk the hallways. My form wasn't the best form, but I felt myself getting stronger by doing it and that's all that I cared about. I was building my stamina again. After my sit ups, I would do what I could remember to work my arm out.

The mandatory "quarantine" set by the state of New Jersey was supposed to be until mid-April. That later got pushed back until almost the end of May. I felt horrible that I just got up and left my home with Brandon. I missed him but knew that this was the best decision for my delicate state at the time. We FaceTimed every night when he got home from work for hours. Since my eye hadn't been stitched for that long, my eye doctor wanted to see me in his office. I remember being terrified about that. A doctor's office?! During COVID?! The germs were probably everywhere! I was afraid to leave the house, let alone be in a small exam room with a doctor. It ended up being fine though and we all wore face masks.

The next week, I was starting to experience horrible pain in my hip and my knee. We set up a virtual appointment with Dr. Cohen, and he suggested getting a brace adjustment. We called the man, Ben, who had created the brace for me. We met with him in a park outside of our house one day so that he could adjust what needed to be adjusted. It turns out that because I had been walking so much, I had actually snapped off a piece of the brace, which explained my hip and knee pain. He had to take my brace back to his office so that he could fix it though, and he brought it back to me the next day.

Ben was the man who was at one point paralyzed from the neck down. Here he was, driving, walking. It was a miracle for me to see that. I wanted to tell him that day that he was my inspiration and his story motivated me, but I didn't say anything. I don't know why. After he left, I was kicking myself for not saying anything to him about it.

Brandon's birthday was April 7, which I missed because of the quarantine. My mom helped me bake cupcakes though and we dropped them off on the doorstep of my house with a balloon for when he got out of work. I was basically in and out of a hospital from September-February, released from the hospital on February 22 and taken from my home on March 16 to quarantine. I was basically home for twenty three days before COVID hit. It was such a blessing to me that I was not in a hospital for all of this though. I don't know what I would have done, truthfully, if I had to be alone in a hospital. My mom was my advocate, especially when I couldn't talk or hear anything that was going on.

In the beginning of May, my sister started to meet us outside during our daily walks to social distance. It was so nice to see her again but I didn't want her anywhere near me! She was treating COVID patients who needed speech therapy after their ventilators were removed. She was one of the COVID heroes but that meant that she needed to keep her distance from me.

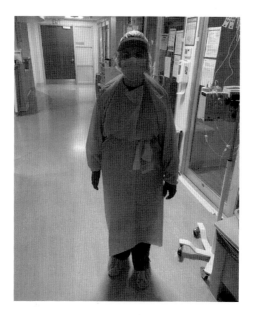

**REBECCA IN FULL GEAR BEFORE
TREATING A COVID PATIENT**

May 17 was Brandon and I's eight year anniversary. He brought Mexican food over and we planned to eat it outside. It was freezing cold and windy though so we decided to set plates up in the hallway of my mom's place. We ate our anniversary dinner in the hallway, six feet apart from each other. Romantic. I know.

As it started to get later in May and the weather started getting warmer out, I would see my dad and sister outside at a park. They would set up beach chairs in a six foot apart circle with me in my wheelchair. From mid-March when we started walking as therapy, until the end of May, I could see little improvements with the way I was walking. I was able to balance a bit better, and I had more stamina than when I first started. We practiced with every device under the sun too- cane, quad cane, one arm crutch, regular walker, rollator walker, hemi walker.

Therapy was still shut down. It was such a shame because I didn't know what I could be doing as exercise besides the few things that I had remembered. I had a few video chats with my speech therapist so that she could see my progress and make sure that I knew what I needed to do, but nothing else. When the end of May rolled around, we got a call that therapy was finally going to reopen again. I was told that I would start working with a new physical therapist that specialized in neuro. I remembered seeing her around the facility before COVID hit so I was excited to start working with her.

CHAPTER 24

The first day back at therapy was very strange. I was required to wear a mask covering my nose and my mouth at all times. Before I saw anyone, the receptionist checked my temperature and asked me a series of questions like if I'd been out of New Jersey, if I have any symptoms of COVID, if I have been exposed to someone diagnosed with COVID recently. They first took my mom's temperature. Ok, cool, 98.4. She then held the contact-less thermometer up to my forehead.

"Umm, it says 100.3. Are you feeling okay?"

I went into absolute panic mode...

"Yeah, I feel fine. I don't understand that."

"No worries, let me take it again." She reached over the table to put the thermometer on my forehead again.

"Hm, still says 100.3."

W. T. F.

"Oh my god, am I sick? What if I get my mom and Mike sick too?" The thoughts came trickling in.

"You're probably just warm on your forehead because you're wearing a hat. Can you try to take her temperature on her neck instead?" My mom asked. We tried it again. I was praying to God that it didn't show up as a fever.

"Okay, there we go. 98.3 You're all good to go."

She gave me a sticker that I put on my shirt that had the date written on it to verify that I was all checked in. I don't know why but I didn't trust the temperature on my neck- I was still scared that I had a fever even though I felt absolutely fine. I saw my occupational therapist first. We pretty much did a new evaluation to record where I was at as a baseline. As she was stretching my arm, she noticed a huge subluxation that developed in my shoulder over the time that I was quarantined.

A subluxation is a partial dislocation. She believed that the reason why this developed was because I was walking every day, but not paying attention to what my arm was doing as I walked. It was kind of just like dead weight hanging there, so after a while, it stretched out the ligaments that held the shoulder in its socket. "Don't worry, we'll do everything we can to try to strengthen your shoulder as much as we can," she said.

I felt like I should have known that I needed to support it. When I touched my right shoulder now, I could feel a big gap between the top of my shoulder and the ball of my shoulder. I couldn't help but think that this could have been prevented if I was in therapy the whole time and COVID was never a thing.

Next, I saw my speech therapist. When she saw me, she was very happy with the progress that I had made. She said that I definitely was able to maintain my progress. I was strict with my home exercise program so I was really glad that she could notice that. We went over a plan moving forward that included sessions with vital stimulation, eating/drinking, voice therapy, and kinesio taping on my face to work on my facial paralysis (all I have to say is thank god for masks).

Lastly, I saw my new physical therapist. She knew exactly who I was and knew all about me. She did a ton of tests with me as a baseline too. She would soon learn that I was a patient who worked her butt off in therapy, never saying no to anything. I was in therapy three days a week for the next few months for three hours a day. New COVID cases seemed to be diminishing as the weather got warmer, so I slowly started going back home with Bran, with family there to help me a lot while he was at work.

More studies about the virus came out showing that it was safe to be outside. Therefore, restaurants all started offering outdoor seating, creating tables in their parking lots. Some had tents too. The first time that I went to outdoor dining was with my sister, her fiancé Chris, and Brandon. We went to a diner with outdoor seating that was next to the highway. I hadn't really been out much to realize what things were like for me now.

I quickly realized that my hearing was a huge issue; I couldn't hear shit. It was one of the first times that I was really out in public too; it was so logistically challenging to figure out where to park and where we were sitting to make it accessible for me. It was also one of the first times out in public with my walker and I had absolutely no balance. I was embarrassed and I knew that people were definitely staring at me stumbling around. I didn't want to look up. Once we made it to our table, ordered, and our food came, the next embarrassing challenge came to light. I couldn't cut my food, so Brandon had to help me.

I also wasn't the cleanest with eating yet- my jaw didn't fully open and half of my face didn't work, so the food hit the outside of my mouth before actually going into my mouth. After every bite, I made sure to wipe my face with a napkin because I knew that I probably had food there that I didn't feel since half of my face was numb also. So that was my first public dining experience. I actually think that it was better being outside because it seemed like there were more distractions around and all eyes weren't on me. Continuing through July was my normal therapy routine, followed by doctors appointments on most days.

JOURNAL ENTRIES

. . . .

Thursday, july 9 2020

This brings me to the present and now to the future of my journey. I thought about how I wanted to continue writing or if I would continue writing at all. I decided that I'm going to start journaling my good days, bad days, all experiences that I'm having and things that I am feeling.

As I look back at the times where I had uncontrollable emotions throughout my story, I can now link it to the cavernoma that was still bleeding in my brain. I don't do that at all anymore, thank God. I also don't need a catheter or a feeding tube anymore either (praise Jesus) and I have no issues with swallowing when eating or drinking. I can even swallow pills now which I was never able to do before! I also realize that during my first stay at rehab, when I developed a facial droop and gnarly headaches that lasted for weeks, it was because I had a stroke, and not one person picked up on it- I was literally in a hospital filled with medical professionals around me and they didn't realize it or believe me. But there's no reason for me to look in the rearview mirror anymore- the only thing I can do is move forward with my life and focus on the important stuff- my recovery.

. . . .

monday, july 13 2020

My occupational therapist told me a few weeks ago about a company that provides service dogs to people who are in need of them at no cost. Service dogs can be extremely pricey. They can be trained to help me with basic tasks like picking up items after I've dropped them on the ground, opening doors, alerting me when alarms go off etc. I applied for this program a couple of weeks ago because I feel like in addition to being helpful for me, a dog would be a great companion to have around. I love pups so much!

The fifteen page online application took me over two hours to complete by typing with a single finger on my left hand. I also had to submit an autobiography and photos with captions. I was so passionate about why I was doing it so I didn't care about the length of time that it took me. I called the organization last week and left them a message to see if they ever received my application because I never received confirmation from them.

Today, I received an email explaining that they are not currently accepting any new applications because of the COVID pandemic. The email also informed me that I should try applying again in a year from now. I was so upset. Getting a service dog was something that I could look forward to after all of this negativity. I'm really bummed that I have to wait at least one year to even apply again, but I just have to roll with the punches that life's throwing. Oh well.

- -

friday, july 24 2020

Tonight was my first time going out with my friends Caitlyn and Megan. Although it was a Friday night, it rained all day so I was hopeful that there wouldn't be a ton of people at the restaurant. I was so self conscious- it was one of my first evenings out and I didn't want to run into anyone that I knew. Normally, I would just walk down the street to meet them, but Mom and Mike had to wheel me to the restaurant. Luckily I had a hat on to hide my short, growing hair and a mask hiding my face.

Mom and Mike spoke with the hostess then rolled me over to an open table. As they were wheeling me past the other tables, I could literally feel people's eyes on me. I mean, I get it. I was always one of those people too that would look at the young person in the wheelchair. I was just curious to know what happened to them and why they were in a wheelchair. I wouldn't be judging them. I just wanted to blend in though. I hated that all eyes were on me. I could feel it and I didn't like it. After a couple of minutes, Cait and Megan showed up.

I just ordered some chips and guac to eat because if I ate anything else, it would just end up all over my face and lap. Even with the chips and guac, I made sure to wipe my mouth after every single bite that I took. It was great to see them both, but I felt so overwhelmed by all of the noise around me. Is this how it's always going to be now? I was embarrassed that I kept having to say "what?" because I could barely hear them with all of the background noise.

After dinner, Cait and Megan wheeled me back to mom and Mike's house. It was very strange to have your friends pilot your wheelchair for the first time LOL. I just made jokes about it. I invited them to hang out at the house for a bit before they left and I'm so glad that I did. We sat at the kitchen table and talked and laughed for hours. I was able to hear them and I was more myself now that I could actually hear. Caitlyn and Megan have always been amazing friends of mine. I met them in college and it was so good for me to just hang out with my girlfriends again. Maybe next time we'll just order takeout somewhere more quiet !!!

. . . .

wednesday, july 29 2020

Today is my 26th birthday. Wow! I freaking made it. I feel like I always knew that I would make it to this day but I'm not sure that I can say the same thing confidently for the people around me. Rebecca, my dad and Brandon took me out for lunch at a restaurant on the water today. I don't get out much these days so I had such a new and special appreciation for little things like watching the boats that sailed by as we ate lunch.

Afterwards, we went to the drive through safari. COVID didn't give us many options for fun things to do. It was difficult for me to see much of what was going on around me, especially with distance, but I made the most of my time. All that really matters at the end of the day is that I made it to my 26th birthday. Thank you God.

. . . .

tuesday, august 18 2020

Today was a jam packed day. I had an appointment with a "movement specialist" at 9:00 AM, then three hours of therapy, followed by another appointment with an or-thopedist. In the last couple of months, I've acquired a tremor in my head that looks a little bit like a Parkinson's tremor. The doctor mentioned that Botox injections could possibly stop the twitching. She also increased the dose of a medication that I was already on. I guess we'll just have to wait and see what happens.

I later went to an orthopedist because I've had the subluxation in my shoulder for months now. I was looking forward to seeing a doctor to finally get this issue addressed. The COVID protocol at most doctors offices now is to park outside, stay in your car and then call the front desk to let them know you are there. Once we called, a woman came out with some paperwork and told us we could go into the waiting room. Shortly after, we went into an exam room. I felt proud of myself because I used my walker to walk in for the first time instead of using my wheelchair.

After about five minutes, the orthopedist knocked at the door. He was in full scrubs, a mask, a face shield, and a netted hair cover. He stood in the doorway- he didn't even come into the room. He basically looked down at my chart and saw that my subluxation was acquired from a neurological condition. Because of that, there was nothing that he could do for me but write up a script for physical therapy. My mom asked if there was any type of brace or support that I could wear and he said no. He literally said to me, "If you fell and hurt your shoulder, I could help you but because you have something neurological, I can't help you. Sorry."

He didn't even come into the room and examine me. It's so incredibly frustrating that nobody has answers for the multiple random issues that I've acquired as a result of what I've been through. Who knew the brain could cause this many problems all over your body that no one can fix. My day ended with a bad mood, until my sister came over with sushi! We just hung out and watched Netflix and ended up having a great night.

. . . .

sunday, august 30 2020

Today was honestly one of the first days where I felt like things were somewhat normal again. I spent the weekend at my beach house in Brigantine, NJ. I had a really long talk with Brandon last night before bed about life and moving forward together- we want to buy our first house togeth-er soon and I'm excited to marry him one day. I love the nights that we can just sit in bed and talk for a while. We hung out on the front porch this morning. I love enjoying my morning coffee with the sun shining and the clouds rolling by. Bran and I stopped in Atlantic City for some lunch before heading home. Sitting there at a table across from him just felt like old times again. I felt like we were on a vacation or something. Driving home felt normal too- al-most made me forget about reality! I need more uplifting and happy days like this- it was a good day!

. . . .

thursday, september 3 2020

I saw a neurologist today for the second time ever. The first time was with the doctor who ordered my original

MRI and today, I saw a new neurologist who can administer Botox injections. After evaluating me, he suggested that I'd get a shot of Botox in my right bicep and two shots of Botox on each side of my neck. The one in my bicep is because I have a lot of muscle tightness in my elbow and it will help relax the muscle and two shots of Botox for my neck because it will help the tremor in my head. I notice the tremor more when I am tired, looking at my phone or when I am stressed out about something.

....

monday, september 7 2020

Today is Labor Day and officially twelve days away from the one year anniversary of finding out that something was on my brain. It makes me really sad to think about that day and the fact that it's coming up so soon. Though things are improving, I thought that I would be much further along by this point. On the contrary, I didn't think that I would need two more surgeries either. We spent this weekend at our house in the Poconos in Pennsylvania. It's a little cabin in the woods on a lake. At first, I was very hesitant to go- what would I do there? I can't paddle board or swim or kayak like I used to. I can't really walk on the hilly grass outside of the house yet either.

My mom waited for me to finish therapy on Friday and we drove up early on Saturday morning. About an hour into the ride, we approached the mountains of Pennsylvania. They were sooo beautiful- even more beautiful then I remembered them being. I used to snowboard in those mountains in the winter. "Wow- I thought that I might have never been able to see the mountains again," I said to my mom, starting to tear up a little. When did I become so corny?! It ended up being a great weekend for me and I was so glad that I pushed myself to go and spend time with Brandon, my mom and Mike, my sister and her fiancé. Very relaxing but the hills were no joke! Let's just say that a lot of physical therapy was done this weekend.

· ·

thursday, september 17 2020

Today is two days away from September 19. I don't know why I am so stuck on this- it's just a day. But I guess to me, it's the day that I lost myself- I lost my identity and I thought I'd have that identity back by now. I am so proud of myself though- today was officially the first time I stayed alone since probably September 19 of last year. I recently discovered that I am able to do my eye drops myself so it gave me the chance to be alone. It's been very difficult for me to do my own eye drops because I have no feeling in my left eye, so I can't feel when a drop goes in. A few days ago, I realized that I can tell when the drop goes in my eye because my vision gets blurry. This was the last thing that kept me from being more independent so the fact that I was able to learn how to put eye drops in myself was a big deal. I use a wheelchair whenever I am by myself at home because God forbid I fall when walking when I am alone; I am not sure what I'd do. I was able to wake up this morning, get dressed, use the bathroom & brush my teeth, make breakfast (from the microwave) and take all of my medicine. From there, it was therapy time. I legitimately do therapy on and off for hours every day. Little things take so much longer for me now, so the day flew by. Before I knew it, Brandon was on his way home from work. Independence feels sooo good.

friday, september 18 2020

As my mom pushed me in my wheelchair to therapy today, I was wheeled past a young boy and his grandmother as they were walking into therapy too. The boy was maybe ten years old, limping heavily and holding his grandmother's hand for support. He also couldn't move his arm or hand on one side and wore a brace on each leg. I felt so sad for this boy. We saw him again after we checked in at the front desk and I honestly couldn't even look at him this time. When we got to the waiting area, I asked my mom if she noticed him and if she thought that he got bullied. "Yeah, I saw him. So sad. I don't know, he might. Kids are very cruel," she said.

Right after hearing her response, I felt tears in my eyes. I just felt so terrible and sad for him. He was so young. Good thing I was wearing a mask and a hat to hide the fact that I was crying. I literally felt a pain in my gut when I was thinking about this little boy and what he had to go through at school with kids who just didn't understand. My already cracked heart cracked a bit more. It really hit me hard, especially now, after being able to relate to him in a way. As the rest of the day passed by me after therapy, I found this little boy from therapy being the thought that kept crossing my mind. I don't know why I can't stop thinking about him, the situation just hurts my heart. Was he born that way? Does he know anything different? He has no idea who I am or that I'm thinking about him or even writing about him, but he gave me motivation. Life must be so difficult for him but if he can do it and push himself, then so can I.

. . . .

saturday, september 19 2020

Wow, the day is finally here. Can't believe this year flew by. I loved that throughout the year, I could look back and say, "this time last year, I was doing x or traveling here." From today on, I can only say that I was in a hospital bed or doing some sort of rehab. It's so surreal to me- I still have to pinch myself that this is actually my reality sometimes. I really thought that I would have made so much more progress at this point but the brain can take a long time. I had a good day today- I went for the longest walk to date with my mom and sister- almost half of a mile!

Tomorrow we get to see my sister's wedding venue. Her wedding date is October 16, 2021. I hate setting dates as goals for myself because I don't want to disappoint myself or rush my healing, but my biggest goal is to be completely healed by my sister's wedding- whatever that may mean for me. I'm her maid of honor, and want to make the day as special as possible with as little attention on me as I can.

. . . .

sunday, september 20 2020

So, I was first admitted to the hospital on 9/19/19. Throughout the last year, my sister and I have been coincidentally seeing 9 or 19 everywhere. Whether my sister looked back at a note that she took at work that was recorded at 9:19 AM or if we got a receipt for $9.19, there were a million random examples of 9 or 19 around us. I googled the meaning of what those numbers meant. It basically said that angel 919 was trying to tell me that they acknowledge that I have been through a major life change, but nothing about what happened in my life was accidental. Nothing was ever taken away from me, but was just making room for something better.

Backtracking a bit but still relevant to the story that I'm about to tell you, my older cousin Jason passed away a couple of years ago. A few months ago, I had a dream that I received a text message from him. Coincidentally, when I woke up the next morning and told my sister about my dream, she told me that it was actually Jason's birthday that day- and I had no idea. Then, my sister had a dream that she saw Jason and asked him if he was the one who was constantly showing us those numbers as a sign, and he said yes.

While I was in the hospital for my surgeries, there was a chaplain named Leah who would come to my room to visit me and share words of encouragement. My family would say that she always knew the right time to come into the room- whether Dr. Brady was telling us about a scan result, or if they were in the middle of making a tough decision about me, Leah would always be in the room. She even found me when my room was down in the ICU. She checked in so much that I don't even remember all of the visits that she gave me.

Fast forward to yesterday, 9/19/20. The one year hospital mark and the date of 9/19. My sister and I were anticipating that we would be receiving a message of some sort on this symbolic day. Nothing ever happened though. Today, my aunt texted me to see how I was feeling (this aunt is Jason's mother). I then received this text from her:

"We have a new Rabbi at our shul. She is a former chaplain at the hospital you were in for your surgeries. We were wondering if you knew her. Her name is Leah. Any chance you know who she is? So lovely!! Stay well sweetie."

The temple where my aunt belongs is probably an hour north of where the hospital was. It was sooo random! Was this just a weird coincidence or was it the sign that I was waiting for? The even weirder part is that my aunt and uncle met Leah for the first time the day prior, which was on 9/19. She virtually held a sermon for the Jewish New Year.

I also realized that 9 was a prominent number in my childhood. My dad and Jason's father had an inside joke since they were young where they called each other "9", the house number that I grew up in was 19, my birthday is on the 29th.

The craziest part of the whole story though was this- my aunt and uncle told me that Leah was planning to host another socially distanced sermon today at the park behind the local high school by their house for Rosh Hashana, the park where my cousin was found when he passed away. I truly believe that Leah was brought to that exact spot for a reason and all of these connections were not a coincidence.

Before my third surgery, my uncle (Jason's father) came to visit me in the ICU. Who came in at the exact time that my uncle was visiting me but Leah! He literally met her. It all just hit me today and I realized that my cousin Jason is one of the strongest spiritual connections and guardian angels of mine that was looking out for me then and was sending me these signs. I also believe that he continues to do so now. It's almost like he brought Leah into my life for a reason, and kept dropping small hints to show me that yes, it was him who had been protecting me. When I was in college, he lived nearby and always made it known that he was around to help me with anything that I needed. It almost felt like the presence of having a big brother. I feel very lucky and safe to know that he will always be with me.

**MY SISTER REBECCA, ME, AND MY COUSIN ELANA
WITH JASON BEHIND US. LOVE YOU JAY!**

saturday, september 26 2020

It's the one year anniversary of my first brain surgery today. I thought that today would make me sad, but instead of being sad, I feel grateful. I am grateful to continue my journey to independence again.

monday, september 28 2020

I had the chance to speak with Eliza and Dr. Brady on the phone today. I haven't been able to see them since my last surgery in December because of COVID- isn't that nuts?! They called me to answer some questions and told me that they are starting to see patients again. I haven't made an appointment yet but I cannot wait to see them! Dr. Brady also expressed concern because I told him that I still had facial paralysis, and it was now nine months post op. He said that we should start looking into having facial reanimation surgery.

To be honest, I don't think it worries me as much as it excites me to potentially have my smile back again, even if that means more major and scary surgery. I have done some research on this type of surgery before and it looks like it has a lot of positive results.

saturday, october 3 2020

Today I saw Lauren, my old roommate, for the first time since rehab last year. We met for a COVID friendly outdoor lunch. She is doing so great, holy shit!! I had no clue if she'd show up in a wheelchair or with a walker but she walked up to the table using just a cane. She is amazing. It was so nice to catch up and laugh about our miserable rehab experience together. She is even starting to drive a little! I have prayed for her a lot and I am so glad to see her kicking butt. I'm so happy that I met her and that she is doing so well.

. . . .

sunday, october 4 2020

I feel really defeated. I want to feel normal and go out with Brandon and our friends. I feel like life is moving around me and I'm just stuck where I'm at. Also, COVID is scaring the shit out of me! Our own president got COVID on Friday. I just don't know what to do anymore. I don't feel comfortable seeing friends indoors but now it's starting to get cold out. I can't go to a loud setting yet because I can't hear very well. Life is just different now and it can be really defeating and lonely sometimes. It's just taking a long time but I know that it will get better eventually.

. . . .

tuesday, october 20 2020

Today I finally got to see Dr. Brady. As we approached the hospital, my stomach dropped. It brought me back to memories that I've been trying to forget. I walked into the office using my rollator walker and waited in the hallway because the waiting room was packed with people and we didn't want to get close to anyone. Dr. Brady walked by and saw me waiting there in the hallway. He lit up like a light!

He ran over to me and gave me the biggest hug. (I was so surprised because with COVID precautions, I didn't think he would want to even be less than 6 feet from me). When we were called to the back, a nurse took my vitals and updated my medication list before he entered the room. I had a big list of questions that I went through and after he answered every question thoroughly, he just chatted with me and wanted to see how I was genuinely handling things both physically and mentally.

We talked for about fifteen minutes. He was so happy just to see me walking. He said that he knew how hard it was for me to be so young, going through something like this and seeing everyone else around me progress in their lives. He always looked out for me. He told me that he wanted me to keep my positive spirit and by doing that I will already win half of the battle.

I was reminded again that there was a time nine months ago that I was basically in a vegetative state, forty or fifty pounds underweight. They almost lost me. I was told to remember that things could always be worse and I have to have gratitude knowing what I am able to do, still making a lot of progress. I have to remember what it could have been. I was lucky to be sitting there in his office, speaking today. He said that I was his inspiration, but he was honestly my inspiration too.

I can't begin to tell you how much I needed to hear that, especially after the last few weeks that I've been having. He said that he was going to have a much better day after seeing me. After hearing his words, it grounded me again. He is the person that my family and I trusted with my life. And he saved my life. For that I am eternally grateful to him.

. . . .

Thursday, october 29 2020

I got the results back from the second follow up MRI that I had done this week. My first MRI from June showed that I still had a large amount of swelling in my brain. Dr. Brady told us that he'd potentially have to put in a shunt in if the swelling didn't dissipate by this scan. When he called me to go over the results today, he couldn't have been more thrilled with what he described. Not only did the fluid drain out from the empty hole where my cavernoma once was, but my brain was now actually starting to regenerate by expanding and growing into that hole. Today my MRI is clear. And looking better and better with each scan. This was the news that I needed to hear today and it totally made me take a step back from little things that I was getting caught up on. At the end of the day, and above all of the hardships that I've faced so far, I was granted a second chance by God and that is what I have to keep remembering.

monday, november 9 2020

Having a very random thought tonight but when I was in high school, some kid who I was "friends with" used to make comments about my nose being big. He literally made me feel like shit and made me feel self conscious about myself. Looking back at photos, I can see now that I was actually a pretty girl and genuinely had nothing to be self conscious about. I also realize that someone like that is not and never was a "friend" to me either. What kind of friend does that?! He might have been kidding... but I clearly didn't take it as a joke if I'm still thinking about it years later.

Today, I looked at his social media page and saw that he is now a psychologist (hmmm, ironic). After seeing what he was up to in life, I decided to remove him as a friend as a way for me to let go of the self conscious thought that I had been holding onto for all of these years and realize that I was always beautiful. I'm not one to hold grudges but I resent him for making me feel horrible about the Rachel who really had no reason to be self conscious at all.

tuesday, november 17 2020

A second wave of the pandemic came on fast and furious this past Friday the 13th. The wave right now is even worse than the one from March. I also was denied coverage for occupational therapy and speech therapy through insurance today which means that every session from now until the end of the year has to be paid for out of pocket. I was also told by my rehab facility that I would only be able to go there once a week instead of my normal three times a week, even though I was willing to pay for three times a week.

One of my therapists told me that I have to remember that at the end of the day, "it's a business too". Really?!? Well it's not a business to me. It's my life. How could they deny coverage to a twenty six year old who still needs to be in therapy? The progress notes that were submitted to insurance stated that I was continually making progress every week. There are so many things right now that are stressing me out, on top of the spiking pandemic.

. . . .

monday, november 30 2020

This weekend, I moved back in with my mom temporarily. For starters, COVID has been raging and since Thanksgiving was this past Thursday, I anticipate that the numbers will jump even higher over the next week or two. Brandon's been starting to go out lately too- I'm uncomfortable being around him if he were to be around a lot of people but I also don't want to stop him from doing that if that's what he wants to do. Now that it's Christmas season, he's even busier than usual, and expected to work longer hours. I don't like that I can't be home, but it just makes sense for me right now to keep myself safe.

· ·

Tuesday, december 9 2020

Tomorrow is the one year anniversary of my second craniotomy. I'm going to try not to think about it too much but it sucks knowing where I am currently at and where I pictured myself being at this point.

I had EMG testing on my face this morning, which measures the nerve activity present. The test showed that the nerve on the left side of my face is "dead" or in other words, unsalvageable; I will definitely need to get facial reanimation surgery if I ever want a chance to get my smile back.

· ·

Thursday, december 17 2020

I received the sweetest gift yesterday that was labeled from the department of neurosurgery wishing me a happy holiday and new year. There were three large boxes filled with fruit and candy. I don't have words to express how kind that was and how much it meant to me. I can't believe that they all thought of me there- they probably have so many patients throughout the year and I felt very special! My heart is bursting with gratitude today.

Totally switching gears here- I started at a new therapy place this week- a place that would allow me to pay to go there as many times as I'd like in a week. This morning, I was in the waiting room next to a man, probably in his forties, who had a large scar on his head. My mom and I started talking to him a bit asking him how he liked the facility and what he was there for. It turns out that a few months prior, he had a seizure that led him to discover a malignant tumor on his brain that was stage three. He said that his doctors told him that if this tumor was stage four, he'd be dead by Christmas.

He is going to undergo both chemotherapy and radiation to treat it. It just goes to show me that although my life may seem so difficult, I am very lucky. Before we started talking, I was sitting there embarrassed to be in my wheelchair, not even knowing what his situation was. I couldn't stop thinking about him all day. His story made me sad. You just never know...

saturday, december 19 2020

So two major drug companies came out with a vaccine that finally got approved for emergency use and they started administering vaccinations to frontline workers last week. It couldn't have come at a better time because the virus is totally out of control after the holidays again. I am scared to take the vaccine myself but am desperate for this BS to just go away.

In other news, I reached a milestone tonight!!! I walked with a quad cane around my house without my mom hovering over me (she was close by just in case though). I am so excited! I hadn't practiced with it in a while and wanted to see if I noticed a difference now from the last time I tried it and I definitely can!!!

. . . .

saturday, december 26 2020

My mom cried to me tonight. I haven't seen her cry one time in the last year. Scratch that- I don't think I've seen her cry ever. I had a bad day today and stormed into my room after telling my mom and Mike that all I wanted to do was go home. I was just sick of quarantining already and it hasn't even been long this time. This was at like 4:00 PM and I didn't leave my room once until almost 8:00 PM to shower (I wouldn't have left my room for the night if it wasn't for my mom making me get up).

My mom was talking to me about how sorry she was that I had to go through something like this, especially during COVID when I couldn't be at home for my recovery. She said that it was okay to have bad days; bad days are better than no days. As she hugged me, I could hear her crying. It really got to me; I love her with all of my heart and I feel so bad that I take out my frustration on her sometimes. She's my backbone.

. . . .

friday, january 1 2021

Happy New Year! Because of COVID, I spent New Years Eve last night by myself in my room. I didn't even know if I'd make it to midnight to be honest. I'm really disappointed because I asked Brandon to get COVID tested so that I could come home for the weekend to spend New Years with him. He never got tested though and went to our friend's house for a party instead.

I didn't write an entry on December 30, the one year anniversary of my third surgery or the "Hail Mary". I had a great day though- my sister surprised me with cake and a balloon- she also pushed me in my wheelchair to the boardwalk so I could see the ocean- it wasn't very cold out that day.

Therapy news: I was planning to have physical and occupational therapy twice a week at my new rehabilitation center, and pay once a week to see my original therapist at the original facility. I was told that I wasn't allowed to pay for visits at more than one place, though. So that idea was squashed quickly. Yeah, crazy, right? I don't really understand it all but all that I do know is that our healthcare system in America is totally fucked. I only have thirty physical therapy sessions covered for the year. How is that supposed to help me? I blow through thirty in a couple of weeks.

Things have been tough on the relationship between Brandon and I. On top of brain surgery and adjusting to my new normal right now, we aren't exactly on the same page with our beliefs when it comes to COVID which makes things all that much harder. I told him that if we could get through everything that happened to me and a global pandemic together, we could take on the world. These times are really challenging our relationship but I know that our love is strong enough to withhold anything thrown our way, no matter how big or small the challenge.

. . . .

wednesday, january 6 2021

Yesterday, I registered for the COVID vaccine. I'm really hoping that I can get it soon. I'm reading a lot about how getting COVID can can affect people neurologically, so I'm terrified!!!! My friend who had a cavernoma removed like me, contracted COVID and just had symptoms similar to a cold. Then, two weeks later, she had a stroke. She's okay, thankfully. But her story is exactly why I need to be extra careful.

. . . .

friday, february 5 2021

Someone referred me to a different rehab facility that specializes in neuro. It's about forty minutes away from my house and accepts my secondary insurance. I had my first session there yesterday and I was pleasantly surprised. They don't have all of the fanciest equipment and machines there, but the therapists are all extremely knowledgeable and hands on. Sometimes, it's more about the quality of your therapist rather than the quantity of equipment that the facility has. I am excited to continue my therapy there.

Also, yesterday, thanks to my sister, I was able to get my first dose of the vaccine, and I had no symptoms at all. Today, I had a sore arm and mild body aches that went away after a few hours. My second shot is scheduled for March 5. I feel so extremely lucky to have been given the opportunity to get the vaccine, especially this early on.

. . . .

monday, february 15 2021

A few months ago, my dad bought me a stationary bike to use for home therapy. When I used it for the first few times this summer, I grew increasingly frustrated with each use. My right foot would just slide right out of the pedal every time I made one full rotation. We actually had to tie my foot down to prevent it from slipping off of the pedal and even then, it would still find a way to slip out. I decided that I was going to leave the bike at my dad's house for a while because I really wasn't able to use it.

Tonight, I was at his house and decided to give the bike another shot. Not only was I able to pedal now but I was on the bike for forty five minutes and my foot didn't slip off the pedal once!!!

The main reason why I am writing this entry today is because I want to share a story- a very crazy story!

Growing up, one of my mom's best friends was a woman named Ronni. Ronni was from Minnesota and was visiting us the week of the September 11 terrorist attacks in 2001. Because of the attacks, all flights were canceled for a while, therefore leaving her stranded at our house for some time. A few years after that trip, she developed breast cancer. After a long battle, she unfortunately lost her life.

Fast forward to a few nights ago, I had a dream that I was talking to Ronni on the phone. In my dream, I knew that she passed away years earlier, but for some reason, it was normal to be talking to her on the phone in heaven. I said to her, "I'm so sorry that most of my memories with you are from when you stayed with us during 9/11 and during such a horrible time in the world." On the other line of the phone, she responded saying, "Oh, don't worry honey. You were very young. It's okay that you remember me and associate our memories with that date because it's how we really got to know each other!" Then, I remember her telling me something about a white Jeep that she was renting.

I had this dream the night before last night and thought nothing of it- I forgot to tell my mom that she was even in my dream. Then today, February 15, I randomly remembered the dream and told my mom about it. It made my mom start thinking about Ronni and sparked her to look up Ronni's obituary from years ago on the internet. She then sent me the link to her obituary in a text that said, "Read the date."

After clicking on the link, my eyes were immediately drawn to the date that she had passed away- February 15, 2012. This exact day, NINE years ago. I then freaked out because not only was today's date a crazy sign from her, but she had passed nine years ago today. My guardian angel Jason always sends me the number nine. I was convinced that it was not a coincidence.

I decided to look into the white car that she mentioned in my dream too. It was basically saying that dreaming of a white car could have two meanings:

1. Control over my life- confirmation that I am on the right path

2. A road to spiritual enlightenment...hmmmmm.

. . . .

friday, february 19 2021

I have had a few consultations with facial reanimation surgeons so far and I have my last one in New York City on Monday with Dr. Owens. I'm excited to meet her and see what she says. I'm in an online group for facial paralysis and I've heard nothing but amazing things about her.

. . . .

monday, february 22 2021

I met with Dr. Owens today and absolutely loved her! I decided that I am going to move forward with her as my surgeon, 100% hands down. She showed more of a sense of urgency too to start the process which is what I'd been wanting. Dr. Owens said that I will need two surgeries- a cross facial nerve graft and a gracilis muscle transfer. A cross facial nerve graft is where she will take the sural nerve from my calf and transplant it from the good side of my face and cross it over my upper lip to the bad side of my face.

After a few months of the nerve growing, I will require a second surgery called a gracilis muscle transfer where she will take the gracilis muscle from my inner thigh and attach it to the nerve in my face. She used the analogy of looking at my nerve like it is an extension cord and looking at the transplanted muscle like the wire that plugs into the extension cord.

We already set up the first surgery- it will be on March 15 at a prestigious hospital on the Upper East side of New York City.

It kind of sucks because with COVID, no one is allowed to visit me- no one is even allowed inside the hospital.

We're going to try to get my mom approved to stay with me by saying that I need the help because I am unable to walk by myself. The first surgery is just a one night stay at the hospital. I was informed that after this first surgery, it will take three to six months for the nerve to grow before I can plan my second surgery. I'm starting to marinate the idea that things may not be better by my sister's wedding in October.

. . . .

tuesday, march 2 2021

My mom took me today to get my first pedicure in over a year and a half! My toes did not really curl either from my tone, so it was great.

. . . .

friday, march 5 2021

I got my second COVID shot today! Now, I only have two more weeks until I am officially vaccinated and safe. I feel so relieved!

. . . .

friday, march 12 2021

This morning, I had a virtual appointment with the ENT who will be assisting with my facial reanimation surgery with Dr. Owens on Monday. His name is Dr. Moore. I assumed that Dr. Moore just wanted to meet me prior to surgery, but he actually wanted to propose an idea to me. He read my case and wanted to implant a hearing device while I was having my cross facial nerve graft done. He said that the incision that they were making for the surgery was the same incision that he would normally make for the implant so it was a no brainer (no pun intended).

Since I have complete hearing loss on my left side, it is a device that gets implanted and screwed onto my skull behind my left ear. It picks up sounds on the left side and sends the vibrations to my inner ear on my right side. It's been really tough trying to adjust to the hearing loss so any procedure that I'm a good candidate for, I'm all for it.

. . . .

saturday, march 13 2021

I'm leaving for the city tomorrow because my surgery is early on Monday morning and we'll be in a hotel tomorrow night. I am worried but I know that I need to do this for a chance to regain my smile back.

. . . .

friday, march 26 2021

My surgery with Dr. Owens was on the 15th and ooof, I'm not going to lie, I was messedddd up from it. I was in some serious pain. This past Wednesday was the first day that I actually started to feel a little bit better. The pain that I had from this surgery was possibly worse than the pain that I had after my craniotomies. I was told that the surgery would be about a half day long. I went in at 8:00 AM and expected to wake up sometime between 12-2:00 PM. My surgery ended up being 10.5 hours long, so I woke up at 7:30 PM. On the first night after my surgery, I didn't feel too much pain in my face. My biggest complaint was my right wrist. It was strapped down during the surgery, but since it stayed in the same position for so many hours, it was extremely stiff and uncomfortable. I honestly felt like it was broken accidentally while I was in surgery. They did an x-ray of my wrist that night, but it luckily showed no sign of a fracture.

I ended up spending two nights at the hospital before continuing my recovery at home. My sister came over on night three which is usually the peak of the pain. I was in so much pain that night that my sister actually passed out from seeing me so uncomfortable. I went back into the city yesterday for a post-op check up and to have my stitches removed. My mom counted the ones on my face and said that there were easily over 70 stitches just there, not including the ones that were on my leg. I have an incision from the tragus of my ear and down two inches onto my neck on both sides of my face, under my chin, under my top lip, on my right calf and on my right ankle. I feel like I already notice more tone and less droop in my face though. I am allowed to go back to therapy on Monday and can't wait to get back to work.

Tuesday, april 13 2021

I went back to NYC today for a follow up with Dr. Owens. Everything is looking good and I am on track for part two of my surgery! She had mentioned an eye surgery to me when I first met her, and today she wanted to schedule a date for it with my new cornea specialist, Dr. Sullivan. I am on the schedule to have a corneal regeneration nerve transplant on May 17 (which is mine and Brandon's nine year anniversary!!) This is a new cutting edge surgery that hasn't been performed very often yet so I believe that they will record this surgery to pave the way for other surgeons in the country and around the world. How cool is that? They basically will harvest the rest of the sural nerve from my calf and thread it from my good cornea in between my eyebrows to my bad cornea (in hopes that it will restore feeling in my eye).

I also had a follow up appointment with Dr. Moore, the doctor who implanted the bone bridge on my skull that will help with my hearing. Today, he was supposed to attach the exterior magnet to the device to activate it. The magnet on the device wasn't strong enough because I still had too much swelling and scar tissue. He has to order a stronger magnet and will mail it out to me as soon as possible. I got very upset though because I was under the impression that the placement of the device would be hidden back in my hair. It turns out that during the surgery, Dr. Moore had to place it directly behind my ear, totally exposed, because the scar tissue from my prior surgeries was in the way of the original placement.

It's so close to the back of my ear that I am not sure if I'm going to be able to wear glasses or a headband and with my hair up, it will definitely be exposed. I guess once the magnet comes in the mail I can play around with it and try to figure it out.

Aside from the placement issue, the actual technology that this device has seems amazing!!! He said that the new model had only been in their office for three days, and I was the second patient to receive it. He also said that I was one of probably five people in New York City to receive this device. I am able to download the app and control the volume on my phone. I'm also able to connect it to my phone via Bluetooth and take calls on it, connect it to my TV to stream sounds, and change the mode of hearing depending on the setting I'm in.

friday, april 16 2021

Today I went to an endocrinologist to address the cyst that was found on my ovaries before all of the craziness started up again with my brain. I honestly just put this on the back burner though because there were so many other things that required more urgent attention… aka my life. On the ultrasound, the cyst that was seen in the emergency room from months earlier had luckily disappeared but she still wanted to put me back on birth control to prevent a new cyst from developing again. She called Dr. Brady first for his approval to put me on a new birth control. He wasn't very fond of that idea though because there was a potential risk of stroke from birth control. They decided that instead of a pill, she would implant an IUD with hormones in it instead.

When my doctor implanted the device today, ho. ly. shit. Is that what a contraction feels like when giving birth? Because if so, I'm not about it. The cramp that it gave me only lasted for a couple of seconds, but my whole body cramped and tensed up. I thought that it'd be nothing because I was used to being catheterized in the hospital so frequently but boy, was it a different feeling and was I wrong!

· ·

sunday, april 18 2021

I got to see my friends today at a backyard BBQ. Most of these friends are couples that Brandon and I are friends with. I haven't really seen them much because of COVID and my situation. Today honestly just made me feel like I was stuck in a time warp and everyone else was moving forward in their lives- it was a really strange feeling. One couple had a baby, another engaged. I am so happy for them and all of the exciting things going on, it just makes me feel sad that I was absent for so long and couldn't be there to celebrate these blessings with them. These are the people that I'm supposed to feel the most comfortable around but I was embarrassed for them to see me like this. None of them made me feel uncomfortable or anything but I just wish that I could just blend in and be the funny, bubbly girl that they all know me to be.

Tuesday, may 11 2021

Can I just say how shocked and disappointed I am at strangers in the world?! If you saw someone who was in a wheelchair or using a cane, how would you act? I would think or hope to think that you'd be respectful, maybe ask them if they need help, maybe not. But at least have some decency, right? I've had not one, not two, but three instances in the last month where strangers weren't kind to me. About a month ago, my sister took me to the department store to get some shorts for summer. As she pushed me into the dressing room, there were two other girls in there, around my age. One of them was using the handicapped room to try on her clothes.

Now don't get me wrong, I totally understand that. The handicapped room was so much bigger- before this happened to me, I would have totally done the same thing. But what pissed me off was that she saw me in a wheelchair, clearly needing the larger dressing room with grab bars and a bench in it, yet she didn't offer me that room. There were like five empty normal dressing rooms next to her. Instead, she pretended to ignore me by staring down at her phone, all while listening to my sister and I struggling to fit my big ass wheelchair in a normal sized room. All while these two idiots totally ignored us. I can't even.

Then, a few weeks ago, I went to the dollar store with my sister. I decided that I wanted to walk into the store with my cane rather than use my wheelchair. I haven't really done that often yet but felt like my stamina has been improving so I wanted to try it. When my right leg gets tired from standing for too long though, it shakes. It's something called clonus. We scanned through some aisles and got what we needed.

My legs were clearly starting to get tired, so we started walking towards the checkout register. Thank God that no one was in front of us so I wouldn't have to stand in a line- I just wanted to get back to the car as quickly as possible since I had nowhere to sit down. With the cane, I walked a bit slower, but we were about four steps away from the checkout line when some rude ass lady jumped in front of us, putting her stuff on the belt. I'm not even exaggerating that we were four steps away- I thought she was joking at first. Like what?!?! I would NEVER do that to someone, using a cane or not.

Ok so now we get to today, my third story about how little hope I have in society. My parents and I went into the city for a pre-op exam with Dr. Owens before my surgery on Monday. Her office is within a hospital, so we had to get a pass at the front desk, and then swipe the pass at a turnstile for little doors to open that we'd walk through. After we talked to the man at the desk and received our passes, we started approaching the turnstile (I was using my cane). We were a couple of feet away from the turnstile when a man came up from my left side, bumped into me, then walked in front of me through the open turnstile. My balance is horrible, so when he bumped me it nearly knocked me off of my feet. And he didn't even acknowledge me. I should have been super dramatic and fallen on the floor or something... Just kidding. So yeah, those are some of my experiences with getting back into public places again. Not the best!! And I'm kind of shocked about that. We are planning to sleep at a hotel in the city on Sunday night for an early morning surgery Monday.

Thursday, may 20 2021

Another day, another note as I am recovering from my fifth major surgery. It was supposed to be five hours, but it ended up taking just over seven hours. This was definitely the easiest surgery that I'm recovering from though. My biggest complaint is that I'm exhausted from the anesthesia. I feel okay, but I look scary! It looks like I got punched in the face in both of my eyes because they are still very swollen and black and blue. I have stitches on both of my eyelids below my eyebrows but they honestly look like they're going to heal very well. I also have an incision behind my knee and another incision about three inches below that where they pulled the rest of my sural nerve.

Dr. Owens and Dr. Sullivan unstitched my eye to transplant the nerve to my cornea, then restitched it closed and implanted a platinum weight in my eyelid. The stitch will help protect the eye for now, and the platinum weight is setting me up for another eye surgery down the road. This future eye surgery will be a strabismus surgery on the muscle of my eye to help with double vision- then they will remove the stitch, opening the eye, and the platinum weight will already be there to weigh the eyelid down so I could close it. I know, so many steps, so confusing. I don't know how long this process will be, but I'm assuming a while.

Back to my surgery from Monday, they were absolutely thrilled afterwards. While I was in recovery, Dr. Owens and Dr. Sullivan told my parents that I was a pioneer. I was the first person, if not one of the first people in New York to have this procedure done. It's so new here. I want to pave the way for other people. I want other surgeons to see their operating technique and learn so that they can help their patients too. And I really am feeling great. No painkillers, barely any Tylenol. This was the easiest recovery that I've had so far.

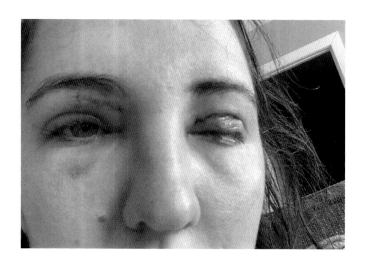

monday, may 24 2021

I feel like I have not written an update about COVID lately. Things seem like they're slowly heading towards normalcy again. Our NJ governor, Phil Murphy, held a press conference today that he will be lifting the indoor mask mandate on Friday. Doctor's offices, airports, warehouses, etc. will still continue the mandatory mask mandate.

I go into the city tomorrow for a follow up with Dr. Owens so that she can remove the stitches from my eyelids and check on my healing eyes. I used to have to take a Xanax whenever they'd remove stitches from the back of my head but at this point, I've had stitches removed so many times from different parts of my body that I'm not even phased by it anymore. Luckily, they glued the incisions behind my legs this time so that there'd be less stitch removal today.

I just want to shout out my mom again. She is amazing and I don't know if I've highlighted her enough on this whole journey. I literally don't know what I would do without her. She dropped her whole life for me. She helps take care of me, attends every doctor's appointment with me, sits in the waiting room alone during 7+ hour surgeries for me (COVID doesn't let others in), drives me to therapy, helps me manage my medication, cooks with me, and schedules doctors appointments for me. She probably does a hundred other things too that I just didn't mention. The true MVP. I have a joke with my family that if someone does a lot to help me with something, I say that they've won employee of the month for that month LOL. If that's the case, my mom wins employee of the month every month for life. She is beyond amazing and I am so grateful for her to be my mom. She is my best friend and I truly couldn't handle my recovery without her. Dr. Brady always told me that I am so lucky to have her, and I know it! During my recent surgery last week, Dr. Owens was saying that as she was operating on me, she kept thinking about my mom.

. . . .

wednesday, may 26 2021

Oh my god! My sister and I went on a Trader Joe's run today (no exaggeration, my favorite store in the entire world). In the middle of shopping, a cashier stopped me with a beautiful bouquet of sunflowers. She informed me that a random customer had bought them for me. No idea who it was but little gestures go a LONG way. That was the kindest thing that a stranger has ever done for me.

....

Tuesday, june 1 2021

This past weekend was Memorial Day. I went up to the Poconos for the weekend with Brandon, my mom, Mike, Rebecca and her fiancé Chris. It was supposed to be the start of summer but it was so cold that we ended up with the fireplace on most of the weekend. Trips like this make me realize that I can't keep up with doing the same stuff that I used to. And it sucks! But when life gives you lemons you have to make lemonade, right? I got help walking down to the lake, exercised a ton, even had help getting into Chris's boat. I remember when I was in the hospital, Eliza kept telling me that I'll have a new normal. Well, for now, this was it. I can't exactly do the same stuff as before, but I can do things in a different way now.

....

Tuesday, june 8 2021

Today I had a last minute appointment with Dr. Brady. I was due for my six month scan last week, and wasn't supposed to have an appointment to go over the results until July. Yesterday, Eliza texted my mom with the results saying, "CT looks stable overall." Then, a half an hour later, his office staff called me and said that there was an opening in his schedule to see me today.

I didn't think anything of it but apparently my family did. They told me that they had a bad feeling that I would be admitted to the hospital again for brain swelling or something. Why else was there this sense of urgency?

It turns out that my scan looked just fine. Dr. Brady and Eliza just wanted to fit me into their schedule a month early so that I wouldn't have to wait that long.

I have been really, really having a hard time this week. It was perfect timing for me to see Dr. Brady to boost my negative mood from turning into a full blown depression. It felt like he was like my life coach or something!

I held it together during the appointment but I was literally crying in the waiting room twenty minutes earlier. The stress that everything's putting on my relationship with Brandon is killing me. It's taking a physical toll on my body- my muscles ache, I can't sleep, my head hurts. Nothing is the same and I can sense him distancing himself from me. Things are so hard; I just want them to get better. I want to be the old me again.

Dr. Brady reminded me that although it's slow, my young brain is resilient and will bounce back- he's confident of that. It might not be tomorrow, or next year. But I have my whole life ahead of me to recover. I just hope that Brandon doesn't become impatient with that. I can't picture my life without him. He means everything to me. Dr. Brady also made a very true statement. I don't have a condition that's going to worsen over time. It is only going to get better over time. He reiterated to me again that I am going to be a mom one day. I can't wait to be a mom one day.

. . . .

Tuesday, june 22 2021

I am waking up this morning and I feel devastated, crushed. I feel like my whole world is spinning. My heart hurts. I had a talk with Brandon yesterday about how he's been feeling- I felt him being distant and wanted to hear what he was thinking. The truth hurts though.

I don't blame him for being afraid of the unknown. There's no book on how to navigate through this with your part-ner, especially when you're so young with so much life ahead of you. I just never painted a picture in my mind of a future without him until yesterday. And I don't know what I would do if that would happen. After our talk, he assured me that he wants to be by my side and is not go-ing anywhere- he just wants to see me get better.

And then this morning, I woke up feeling horrible. It's just the seed that was planted in my head yesterday afternoon that scared me so much. Partly, I think it has to do with my insecurity. Because of that, I do everything I can around the house to make life easier for him when he gets home from work. I am doing everything that I am physically able to do right now to contribute to my relationship. I can only hope that it's enough though and he sees that I'm trying the best that I can. I just don't know how to feel about it all. Everything that has happened to me has ruined my life in every aspect. I still can't wrap my head around it all. I just want to get better and get my life back.

· ·

Tuesday, july 6 2021

I spent the long holiday weekend in Brigantine. It was a nice weekend- I even reached the new milestone of being able to go on the beach. Although it wasn't pretty, I did it. And that's all that matters, right?

So I joined this online group last year for people who have brain stem cavernomas like me and I met someone named Javier. He is around my age and went through three surgeries like me too. We talk from time to time but it was crazy how similar we were. I never met anyone who had basically had all of the same residual symptoms as me. It was nice having someone to talk to that just gets me. He's from Pittsburgh but reached out to me because he was visiting a friend in New Jersey this weekend and wanted to see if he and his parents could stop by our house to meet. Javier and his parents were such great people! To meet him in person was actually surreal. He was such an inspiration for what I want to be in the future as I recover and his attitude towards everything that has happened to him was so powerful and contagious. He just owned it.

Meeting him and hearing about him really reminded me of my story. It was nice for our families to talk too because not many other people can truly understand what we all went through except for us. We all had so much in common with each other. Before they left, Javier gave me a gift with a few things in it. He handed me the bag, then automatically knew to assist me with opening the stuff in it because of the struggle with using one hand. It really stuck out that we kind of had an unspoken language. He knew right away what it was like and knew to assist with something like that.

After Javier left, I found myself thinking about him a lot- he really touched my heart and left a mark on me because I can really understand him and his struggles on a different level. He gives me hope as I slowly progress in my recovery. The way that I felt when we met Javi this weekend was probably the same way that people feel when they meet me. I never thought that I'd have the opportunity to understand that feeling. It was so cool. I feel so lucky to have him as my friend as I navigate my brain's recovery.

monday, july 12 2021

This weekend was the first time that I touched the ocean water since 2019. I hobbled my way onto the beach, I hobbled my way to the shoreline, and I sat on my beach chair while the waves rolled in onto my feet. It was truly bliss. I could never have dreamed of doing that last year. I'm happy to be given the chance to do that again.

For a while, I was ashamed of myself and embarrassed to do things in public. I don't know what changed in me, but now I couldn't give a shit less. I'm going to go out and enjoy doing things that I like and want to do. I'm not going to sit inside because I'm embarrassed. I'm going to live and enjoy my life. If people judge me...shame on them. They have no idea what I've been through or how far I've come so far.

wednesday, july 21 2021

I had an appointment for my fourth round of Botox on Monday. I've been seeing a new doctor for this who I absolutely love. He has more equipment to monitor the injections that he gives and tracks the amount of Botox that is injected into each body part. Botox is injected into the muscle surrounding my shoulder, elbow, wrist, fingers, thigh, ankle, foot, toes- I basically need it everywhere so

I should probably just start drinking it. Then, yesterday, I went to the city for a follow up with my corneal specialist, Dr. Sullivan and my facial surgeon, Dr. Owens. The appointment with Dr. Sullivan went well.

My appointment with Dr. Owens went great too. She is very pleased with how I healed from my first nerve surgery in March and she said that I am ready for the second surgery (the gracilis muscle transfer). We booked a surgery date of September 1 which kind of sucks because I'm planning my sister's bridal shower which is on September 12- but hopefully I'll be feeling alright! This will be an all day surgery at the same upper east side hospital in NYC. I will have to stay in the hospital for five nights afterwards this time to be monitored to make sure that the muscle does not clot off and blood continues to flow through it.

Last night, I started feeling a little under the weather and then I woke up this morning feeling like I got hit by a truck. I feel feverish, I have body aches, a runny nose, sneezing, headache, and congestion. And then I remembered that after my first round of Botox last year, the same thing happened to me. Apparently it can be an immune response to the Botox that triggers flu-like symptoms... oooooh, lucky me. It's weird because I didn't respond like this after my second or third round of Botox, but the good thing about this is that I know symptoms will subside tomorrow or Friday at the latest.

monday, august 8 2021

I had my monthly evaluation in physical therapy today to track my progress. Last month, I stood for thirty eight seconds during my balance test and today I stood for forty eight seconds! I also do another test where I walk for six minutes and we track how far I can walk during that time. Last month I walked 460 yards and today I walked 520 yards. The numbers don't lie. The changes that I continually feel are actually changes happening.

wednesday, august 11 2021

We got a call from Dr Owen's office that there was a scheduling conflict and my September 1 gracilis muscle surgery needed to be moved. Things in the fall are so hectic with events around my sister's wedding so I can't push that September 1 date at all. I decided to schedule the new surgery date for October 20, four days after my sister's wedding. At first I was super bummed because I really just wanted to get this surgery done and over with but then I realized how many things I am now able to attend now that I wasn't able to before. My cousin is getting married in New York the last week of August, my other cousin's baby girl is getting baptized on September 5, my sister's bridal shower is September 12, her bachelorette party is September 17, and my sister's wedding is on

October 16! Busy, busy, busy, but hopefully the fall will buzz by and surgery will be here before I know it.

. . . .

monday, august 30 2021

I just got home from my cousin's wedding weekend. It was so much fun! The last time I saw family was either when they came to visit me in rehab in early 2020, or prior to any of my brain surgeries. Because everyone was basically locked down from COVID, it almost felt like a reunion to see my whole family again.

The wedding was so beautiful. At the reception, the first song that I heard the band playing was "My Girl" and it didn't take much convincing for me to get Brandon to get up and dance with me. Since it was the first event that I have been to since everything happened, I was nervous about how it would go. Although my balance wasn't the best, Brandon made it easy for me to forget about that and just have fun.

After a minute or two into the song, I noticed that my aunts and uncles came to the dance floor, putting their arms around each other in a circle around Brandon and I. They danced with us, and they were all crying... happy tears though!!! They all hugged me and told me how much they loved me when the song was over. That moment was so beautiful to me. They didn't have to say much to show me how proud they all were of me. I know it has been quite some time since my family has seen me prior to this weekend, and I'm sure they didn't know what to expect. I think that seeing me on the dance floor far exceeded their expectations and I was proud to show them how far I've come so far.

. . . .

sunday, september 5 2021

Today was my niece's baptism- her name is Layla Rose and she is a complete angel on earth. Meeting Layla is teaching me how lucky I am to be alive to watch her grow up, witness her baptism, and be there for more of her important life milestones. I love you sweet girl!

· ·

thursday, september 30 2021

I got my COVID booster shot yesterday. My doctor wanted me to have it before my sister's wedding on the 16
and before my major part two surgery on the 20.

I haven't gotten around to writing any entries in a little while because I just haven't been in the mood to.
Brandon expressed to me a little over a week ago that
he wanted to take a break. A break to work on ourselves and try to mend our broken relationship. Nine
years together is something that we don't want to just
give up on but it hasn't been easy. We're planning to
see each other again prior to my sister's wedding and
hopefully attend it together. I also forgot to mention
that September 26 was the two year anniversary of my
first surgery. I can't believe two years have gone by, but
I am pretty proud of the progress that I have been able
to make in that time.

· ·

friday, october 8 2021

Well, tonight, Brandon broke up with me. My heart is shat-
tered. I don't really have much to say honestly. What can
I say? I actually saw a photo yesterday though from my
first trip to rehab. Those weeks were easily the toughest

weeks of my life. Seeing that photo signifies that I am strong and signifies that I can get through anything.

In addition to that, I have really been doing positive things for myself these last few weeks. I've been going on the stationary bike and working out everyday, I signed up for a virtual yoga program, I sent in my application for a service dog again and I went to an expo all about adaptive equipment, devices and things that can help people to navigate through life easier. I have also been living at my house on my own the last few weeks.

Yeah this sucks and it's probably going to be miserable but I am still living and I'm proving to myself that I can live on my own here or anywhere. I'm not going to let my emotions take over and control how I recover from here on out. I'll be damned if I let them. I have to be in a good place mentally with my surgery coming up. If anything, my pain will turn into power and motivate me further to get better and prove that I can do it all by my freaking self.

My sister's wedding is a week from tomorrow and Brandon said that he would still like to go and be my date. As of right now, I'm really not sure what I would like to do. I think I need a few more days to process my feelings before I make a decision. Regardless of what happens between him and I, he was my high school sweetheart, my first love. I don't want things to go bad. I just have to protect my own heart and do what is best for me.

. . . .

Tuesday, October 12 2021

I made the decision yesterday that I don't want Brandon coming to my sister's wedding. It was really tough for me to make that call and I was going back and forth but I didn't want this weekend to make things feel normal, therefore confusing me for the final days before my surgery and before he went on vacation to Las Vegas.

I also want Rebecca's wedding day to be about her and don't want to take anything away from that. My mind has to be in the best place before getting this surgery so I think that I made the right decision. Bran and I are hopeful that taking time apart now will allow us to both work on ourselves. It's crazy to even write that we're not together…

Rebecca's wedding is officially four days away though! Woo hoo! For the longest time, I remember writing about how I wanted to walk by the time of her wedding, have my eye unstitched, have my face back to normal. Honestly, none of those things have happened yet but honestly, I really don't care anymore. I've come to terms with it and have realized that true beauty lies from within and my appearance is just a shell of what actually really matters. My personality is what makes me awesome. First of all, my humor is unmatched. Kidding, kind of. Being a good person, having a good heart, having a good head on my shoulders, being a caring friend, showing resilience, being strong AF- all qualities that matter.

I have always pictured Rebecca's wedding day completely differently for the last two years. I would daydream about my beautiful, symmetric face, walking down the aisle hand in hand with my boyfriend. But things are going to be much different than how I pictured them to be. My strength can and will get me through this tough time though. God is on my side and He will provide me with the strength that I need.

. . . .

monday, october 18 2021

We just got home from Rebecca's wedding yesterday and the entire weekend exceeded my expectations. It was amazing!! My mom and Mike walked me into the ceremony and then the rest of the night I was independently using my walker to get around the venue. Our morning started at 8:00 AM and I didn't leave the after-party until like 1:30 AM so I am still so exhausted today as I write this. I was so worried about giving my maid of honor speech because I was afraid of how my voice sounded to other people since I haven't had my surgery yet. I practiced reading my speech aloud and recorded myself reciting it so many times over the last few months.

I delivered it perfectly on Saturday! The key was speaking loud and slow. People were cracking up at some of the jokes that I told about my sister, like how she asked if I came out black or white after I was born or how I realized that she is actually freaking hilarious after I had three brain surgeries. What this day showed me though was that there are sooo many people in my life that care about me and love me. They had about 130 guests present and it was so nice to know that all of those family members and friends are people that were rooting for me, love me unconditionally and just want the very best for me. Of course, this day was all about my sister and her hubs, but it also made me feel good just knowing how many people are in all of our lives.

DELIVERING MY MAID OF HONOR SPEECH TO REBECCA AND CHRIS AT THEIR WEDDING

My angel, Jason, was with us this weekend too. On Friday night, a lot of the guys in my family went down to the lobby of the hotel to play poker. They were deciding how much each chip should be worth after dealing out chips per player. They decided to make each chip worth 25 cents. They realized that the total per person when they added it up was $9.00.

Then, today, I had another really crazy and random realization! My two lucky numbers are 15 and 21. When I used to play soccer, I always wore the number 15 or 21. Then, when I went to rehab, my room number was 1520-001. All of my passwords contain 1521 and even the lock screen of my phone is 1521. Today I realized that 1+5+2+1= 9. I can't believe I just realized that!

Tomorrow, I am leaving for the city. We are staying in a hotel tomorrow night, and my surgery is early on Wednesday morning. At my pre-op appointment with Dr. Owens, she said that it will likely be an all day procedure somewhere between 6-10 hours. I have been working on belly breathing as much as possible to expand my lung capacity since I tend to get pretty short of breath especially after many hours of anesthesia. I am not afraid of this surgery at all though. I am hopeful and ready to put it behind me. I'm ready to go and get it over with.

. . . .

Tuesday, october 26 2021

I had my gracilis surgery last Wednesday, October 20. I'm writing this while I'm currently still in my hospital bed. My surgery ended up being fourteen hours last week- Dr. Owens is a saint. Post-op, I was moved to the ICU and stayed there for three nights. Then I was moved to a "step down room" which has less around the clock nursing than the ICU but more care than a normal room. I'm in a step down room now. There are two things that I remember from the morning of my surgery-

1. The song that was playing while I was laying on the operating table about to be put to sleep- Levitating by Dua Lipa.

2. The feeling that I had after waking up from fourteen hours of general anesthesia. From my point of view, my room in the ICU was flipped ¼ of the way around. The ceiling tiles were on the left wall and the privacy curtain that was supposed to be to my right was on the ceiling. I felt so discombobulated, like I was going to topple over the ledge of my bed rail while lying there.

My mom had special permission by the hospital to stay with me, and my dad and Mike were nearby at a hotel, planning to visit when they were allowed to, based on the COVID restrictions that the hospital had in place.

The night before my surgery, I went to an Italian restaurant in the city with my dad that was a few blocks away from our hotel. It was a nice night so we decided to eat outside. While we were in the middle of our dinner, I noticed that dad had a little cough and he told me that he felt a little short of breath. Anybody who knows me knows how neurotic I am about germs.

"Dad, you know that those are COVID symptoms right?"

"Yeah but I'm fine, Ray. Don't be crazy!"

"Ok well COVID or not, I am having major surgery tomorrow so maybe we should be wearing masks. I'm not trying to catch anything."

After we ate dinner, we put our masks on, went back and hung out in his hotel room for a little while, then I went back to my mom and Mike's room to get some sleep before my 5:00 AM surgery morning.

My dad met my mom, Mike and I in the hotel lobby the morning of my surgery. It was so early that the sun wasn't even up yet and there was a chill in the air. Mike sent my mom, dad and I off in a taxi that was heading to the hospital. Since it was so early, all of the New York City streets were empty. When we got to the Upper East side hospital, I signed a bunch of papers, then waited about twenty minutes until my name was called. I then gave my dad a hug goodbye.

"Good luck Ray, I'll see if I'm allowed to see you in the recovery area later. Otherwise, I will just see you tomorrow. Love you, good luck!" Fast forward to about 11:00 PM the night that surgery was over, I found out that a bridesmaid and two groomsmen from my sister's wedding (a few days prior) had tested positive for COVID. I then remembered that my dad didn't feel good the night earlier when I was at dinner with him. I didn't know how to process this news... I was super concerned and pretty freaked out!

I knew that I was afraid of getting COVID in the first place because of how it could affect me and my brain, but now, I was also very weak because of my long surgery and my breathing was so shallow. I was also pretty concerned about my dad. Apparently, while I was in the operating room, my parents were notified about the positive cases. From the city that day, my dad, Mike, and my mom all went to get tested. All three of their rapid tests came back negative, but my dad felt even worse than the day before. While I was still in surgery, he decided to drive back home to Jersey.

My mom called Dr. Owen's office to let her staff know about the situation and urged them to COVID test me while I was under the knife. I don't think that her and her team ever tested me though because they didn't have my consent to do it. It seems as if I missed a lot of drama while I was sleeping, huh, LOL.

By the time that I was really awake and alert, it was 11:00 PM and time for bed. My only complaint that night was about my blood pressure cuff on my arm- it went off every few minutes to get my pressure and squeezed the shit out of my arm while I was trying to sleep. The other thing that bothered me was that I was catheterized during surgery, and they left the catheter in for the night.

I'm such a weirdo; it wasn't the actual catheter that bothered me- it was the bag where my urine went. For some reason, they had the bag in my bed with me so every time that I would pee, I felt the warm bag filling up beside me on my leg and thought that it was leaking pee on my bed... I finally had my nurse move it to the floor though, thank god.

Because I had a muscle transplant, the nurses had to monitor the muscle in my face every hour, meaning that I really didn't get much sleep.

They had to do two "internal and external doppler checks" each hour where nurses would, in essence, ultrasound my face to listen for the blood flow going to the newly transplanted gracilis muscle. I was soooo thirsty and soooo hungry because I hadn't eaten anything since the night before my surgery.

When I woke up on Thursday morning, one day post-op, I was hoping to be able to eat and drink something, but the residents that morning told me that I was not allowed to eat/drink yet, just in case the doppler showed that the muscle didn't have blood flowing to it and emergency surgery was needed. I was more awake now, so I was able to see and feel all of the surgical sites.

My groin on my left leg had a 3.5 inch incision where they took the gracilis muscle and it had a drain above it for postoperative fluid. I had a second incision on my left thigh that was about an inch long, and a third incision that was identical to that which was about 3.5 inches below it. A second drain was here too.

I had stitches around my left nostril and stitches from my left earlobe, down my neck, with a third drain popping out from my neck. This is what they referred to as my "flap". Literally... cutting my face open by my ear as a flap, planting the muscle, and stitching it back up. My left eye was also black and blue. Definitely not a cute look for me. I was intubated for so long during the surgery that my throat hurt and it was super dry. I felt pain and pressure on my surgical sites but was honestly so distracted by how hungry and thirsty I was that it kept my mind off of any major pain temporarily.

My dad called me on Thursday morning and told me about his cough, chills, shortness of breath, body aches, and now, fever. He was going to an urgent care again that was close to home to get retested. A half an hour later, he texted me that his rapid COVID test came back positive. Oh no.

On the phone with him, I could hear in his voice how sick he was. It came on sooo fast though- I was with him the morning earlier and he seemed alright. He told me that he was just going to go to sleep for a while. I was hoping that at some point on Thursday, I'd be able to at least drink some water, but I was wrong. I was so hungry too.

The doppler checks were still every hour on my face and things were looking good though. Thursday night, my temperature was 99.5. I was freaking out because the low fever could be from the anesthesia, but it could also be the start of COVID. I was coughing a lot, but that could have also been from the intubation and irritation on my lungs. The last symptom that scared me was my breathing. It was extremely shallow and my voice was hoarse when I spoke. This also easily could have been from a days worth of anesthesia and intubation but I just didn't know.

Friday, my temperature in the morning was back to normal and they allowed me to start having liquids, but still no food. I was able to have clear juice, broth, jello- basically stuff that you'd have for a colonoscopy prep. My dad called me on Friday afternoon and told me that he was going to the emergency room to get the IV antibody COVID treatment. This was supposed to help shorten and lessen the symptoms and help you fight it off quicker. Because I was directly exposed to someone who had now tested positive, my nurses swabbed me and told me that I would just have to wear a mask whenever anyone came into my room until I got my test results back. It wasn't so easy to put a mask on though- my face had just been operated on. It wasn't fun.

With my doppler checks, things were looking good so all of the checks got spaced out to every two hours instead of one. I heard from my dad on Friday evening that he was home and resting after the treatment from the emergency room. He was vaccinated in March, but hadn't had a booster shot yet (I did). I wasn't sure if that could have been part of the reason why he got it- my theory was that his vaccination had faded since March and he was due for his booster.

Friday night, when the tech took my temperature again, it was 99.6. I was terrified and worried about it again all night. Could this be the start of something? Saturday morning, my temperature was normal again, and my COVID test came back negative. I was also finally able to start eating solid food. I wanted to just stuff my face but I really hadn't had anything in my stomach since Tuesday night, so I knew to take it very slow. Food tasted amazinggggg.

On Saturday, I was transferred out of the ICU. Looking at my reflection was scary though- I looked so messed up and one side of my face looked like a chipmunk. Dr. Owens warned me that the gracilis muscle would be very bulky at first and needed time to atrophy down to its normal size. It was also so swollen. On Sunday morning, the residents finally removed the drain from my neck, but told me that the two drains in my leg would have to stay a few days longer because they were still producing a lot of fluid.

NFL Sunday occupied most of my day. The Giants basically shut out their opponent. Very entertaining Sunday for me. My mom and I also ordered pizza to the room.

New York pizza is good but nothing can beat NJ pizza if I'm being honest.

Yesterday and today blurred together. The days seemed identical because time was just dragging on. Yesterday morning, I was pleasantly woken up at 6:30 AM by a woman from the lab who was looking to prick me to get a sample of my blood. Then, ten minutes later, the residents came to my room to check on me. Apparently, I had staples or something that felt similar to staples on my collarbone that didn't need to be there anymore because they ripped them out one by one. Lovely. Holy shit, owww?? There were only a few staples but I didn't even know that they were there. I went back to bed for a little while after that.

I spoke with my dad when I woke back up and he is feeling a lot better now, finally, but he still has to quarantine until the CDC recommendations say that he is able to get back into society- I think it's ten days after positive test results. I am currently waiting for the residents to come into my room this morning, hopefully remove the stitches from my face and the two remaining drains from my leg, and discharge me to go home.

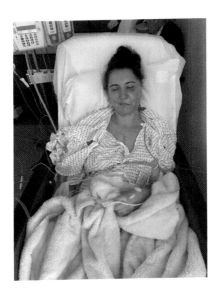

**AFTER MY SECOND FACIAL SURGERY. DEFINITELY
NOT THE MOST FLATTERING PHOTO BUT YOU
GET THE IDEA... IT WAS VERY INVASIVE LOL**

Thursday, october 28 2021

I am in the car and am FINALLY on my way home from
the city! I can't wait to see my kitten and take a nap in my
own bed. On Tuesday after my journal entry, a resident
came to my room and removed every other stitch on my
neck/ear, but said that the stitches by my nose were not
ready to be taken out yet and needed a few more days to
close up. He also said that the two drains in my legs were
still producing a lot of fluid and he wanted to keep them
in for a few more days. I was still going to get discharged
from the hospital though.

Instead of driving back to New Jersey and then back to the city a day later, my mom, Mike and I got a hotel room in the city on Tuesday night and Wednesday night. We got to the hotel room around 2:30 PM on Tuesday- I literally went straight to the hotel bed and knocked out until 6:00 PM. I think that was the first time I slept for that long, uninterrupted, all week. I stayed in the room, resting, all day Wednesday, and we went to Dr. Owen's office this morning at 9:00 AM for my follow up appointment.

Overall, she was very pleased with how well I was healing. She removed the stitches around my nose and from my ear to my neck. She also removed one of the drains from my thigh. There was still a second drain in my groin, but it was draining a lot so she wanted to keep that one in. She said that we could remove it after the weekend.

My cheek where the muscle was planted looks like I pumped a ton of air in it or a bee that I was allergic to stung me ten times. It's really, really big. She said again that this was totally normal and part of the healing process though. I'm just going to trust her and plan to hide from society until further notice !!!

This week gave me a lot of time to reflect on everything going on with life in general. So many emotions have overcome me- sadness, loneliness, and now, anger too. I also think it's really shitty that some people who claimed to be "friends" of mine knew what was happening between Brandon and I, knew about my upcoming surgery but never reached out to me once. Not a call, text, nothing through social media. Why am I so good to people who aren't in return?

I don't need anyone or anything controlling my happiness. I'm strong AF and I can do this all by myself. Screw people that don't bring good energy into my life. My mom and I were also reflecting on what the hell has happened in my life over the past two years. In under two years, I have had six MAJOR surgeries. I was trying to count all of the scars on my body. I think I'm at eighteen different scars right now, with a few more possibilities for more surgery and scars down the road.

It's funny because when Dr. Brady completed my first brain surgery, the incision that he made was right along my hairline and it was basically hidden. I was kind of pissed about it at the time because I was proud of my scar and wanted to show off my battle wound. Now, I have too many battle wounds to keep track of all over my freaking body.

. . . .

monday, november 1 2021

It's 5:00 AM. I'm sick to my stomach and I can't go back to sleep. My mind's racing all over the place. I know that I haven't really shared much about what's really happening in my relationship as of recently but some things are just better left unsaid and it's not right if I were to paint a picture a certain way. I just went back and read a few journal entries from the past few months though and it's really giving me the ability to see my life from the outside looking in- why was I trying to hold onto something so badly?

I don't have to prove anything by being able to do certain things. I've said it before and I'll say it again and again- I have been dealt a really shitty hand- I just have to figure out how to move forward and live a happy life now. I was talking to Javi the other day and said that I didn't know why God was trying to punish me. He responded by saying, "He's not punishing you because he saved you and saved you for a reason." And that hit me sooo hard. Life is so much bigger than a break up, or a surgery, or even just a bad day. And I was embarrassed to be complaining about it because he was so right. Out of all people, he was a friend that could genuinely relate to me and understand the feelings that I was having.

. . . .

wednesday, november 17 2021

I've been trying to keep busy and I would say that I am being pretty successful at it. I decided to organize a coat drive to benefit one of the local charities here in New Jersey. It will run through the month of November and so far I've collected twenty jackets. Tomorrow, I am going back to my old office for the first time to surprise my co-workers. I was planning to do this for sooo long, but with COVID, the office was shut down for a while. I know that they have told me in the past that they would hire me back whenever I am ready to come back, but I think I still need some more time. I know that I definitely could not do the job that I used to do.

My company has been so good to me over the last two years though. When I was in the hospital, they would send over our Chief Medical Officer to visit me. He came on multiple occasions. He would even talk to Dr. Brady about my medical care plan. My department also organized a day where they went to our professional studio in the other office to shoot a video to send to me to keep me in good spirits while in the hospital. I'm really excited to go back to surprise some of my old friends- I don't even know who works there anymore!

A realtor also came to assess the house that I'm currently living in. I've lived here since I was twelve years old with my mom and my sister. My sister moved out when she went away to college, then my mom moved out when I went away to college. After I graduated, I moved back in here with Brandon. We've lived here together for the last five years.

As of right now, I am not sure where or when I am going to move. This house is going on the market in the beginning of December. The housing market is crazy right now and I think that I might just take a few months to wait it out and live with my mom or dad. I had another round of Botox done yesterday too. I was definitely due for it because every muscle throughout my arm feels extremely tight- especially my hand and fingers.

I'm excited because I'm going to Rhode Island this weekend to see my cousin's new house. My niece, Layla, will be there too and I'm so excited to squeeze her lil cheeks! My family is seriously the best- they all make me feel so happy and loved! On Wednesday, I am going to the Poconos for Thanksgiving with my mom, Mike, my cousin, her husband and their two kiddos. I'm so excited to have a low key, chill weekend with the family! I'm all about these vibes.

. . . .

wednesday, november 24 2021

Well it's another 5:00 AM entry. I've been tossing and turning for the past two hours and finally caved and decided to look at my phone. I am so heartbroken- I honestly don't know how I am going to get myself through this challenging time. I don't sleep well at night, I'm not eating great, I always have a headache and I cry at random times. I need to figure out how I can refocus my energy on the positive stuff going on in my life- it's just really hard for me right now. In a couple of hours, I am leaving for the Poconos. Hopefully I can enjoy my time there and have a nice weekend.

Bran packed up and took the rest of his things last night. We also decided that he was going to take our cat because she is technically his cat even though I call her my child LOL. It's weird because Maui was never allowed in our room so we always kept our bedroom door closed. This is the first night in five years that I slept with the bedroom door open. It's weird as hell and feels really empty here.

A lot of the furniture here at the house is gone too. It's sad because we were looking to buy a house together. We had a realtor and everything- I just always thought that moving out of this house would mean moving to a house of our own together. The day after I get home from the Poconos, I am moving out of this house. I'm going to live at my dad's house for about ten days. Then, my mom, Mike and I are heading south for a while.

While we're gone, the townhouse that I live in is going on the market. I was unsure of where I was going to live when I got back. My sister and brother-in-law have been trying to buy a house for literally years with this insane housing market. A few weeks ago, they went to a random open house that had a private apartment on the lower level with its own entrance. They weren't looking for a mother-daughter house but they fell in love with it, put an offer in and got the house. After I get back home, I am going to move into that apartment at their house for a while. God works in mysterious ways and I am really grateful for that. I know that eventually I will be okay. I just wish that I could fast forward and be okay now.

saturday, november 27 2021

I just got back from a great weekend in the Poconos for Thanksgiving. I honestly had such a nice weekend. Family is so important to me. My cousin and I had a long talk last night and I'm feeling so much better and refreshed about the things in life that were making me sad. My happiness has to be put first and I need to find things that will fuel my happiness. I also noticed some major positive changes this weekend.

For starters, I used to have to wake up early to take my medicine for nystagmus and even then, my eyes would still jump pretty bad for hours afterwards. I noticed this weekend that I'm not as reliant on my medication first thing in the morning anymore. My eyes still do jump but it's a lot more tolerable than it used to be. Also, it's hard to explain it but when I walk on the carpet, I am usually so unstable. I guess the plush carpet feels like a balance board to me. It's so insane how my brain recognizes the slightest change in a walking surface. Anyway, the last time that I was in the Poconos, I was falling all over the place because of the carpeted floors. This weekend, although I was a little wobbly, I just walked slowly with my cane and didn't fall over one time.

My nephew is four and was doing a card trick with me. I had to pick a random card from the deck. What number did I pick? A freaking nine. Then after the trick was over, he had me pick a new card. It was number nine, AGAIN! Jason was with me this weekend, I know it. I think aside from looking out for me during my surgeries, he is now looking out for me and my mental health. Making sure that I stay positive and pick my head up when I need to. That I don't get off track with what I really need to focus on- a healing, stress free, happy life. He's shown me that he's still there, looking out for me like a big brother would do.

. . . .

monday, november 29 2021

I finished collecting coats today for my coat drive! There were a total of fifty eight jackets donated over the past month. I'm so happy to be able to provide these to a local charity to give to the homeless this winter. I also decided that I'm going to start volunteering at an animal shelter in my free time. I'm moving into my dad's house tomorrow until my sister's house is ready. Sooo many changes are going on in my life right now- I can't wait to be settled in somewhere.

On my way to therapy this morning, I was telling my mom about my improving nystagmus. She had me look into her eyes because she can usually see my pupils jumping all over the place, but she said that she noticed a BIG difference too. A lot less shaking. She even said that maybe in the spring or so next year, I can start looking into driving an adaptive car again. In therapy today, I was on the treadmill and got up to the fastest speed to date. It's really cool to see slow, little, positive changes like that.

. . . .

monday, december 27 2021

This past month, I have been doing so great. I'm finding my motivation again. I'm focusing on me, my happiness and my healing body. I'm learning to love myself and accept my new self and my new life. I'm embracing it all and not feeling the pressure of being on any sort of timeline, I'm just being and living day by day. I'm focusing on fueling my body with healthy food and working out. And I'm slowly seeing the positive changes. My hair is FINALLY long enough for a bun now too.

My balance and walking are improving, the strength in my legs is getting better. I can walk long distances and stand for long periods of time without my legs shaking from being tired. I'm starting to notice more symmetry in my face at rest. The muscle from my surgery is finally starting to atrophy down.

I am meeting with Dr. Sullivan in early March and I'm assuming that we're almost ready to remove the tarsorrhaphy on my eye and possibly plan a strabismus surgery. The two year anniversary of my third brain surgery is on Thursday. This isn't a day for me to be sad, it's a day for me to celebrate being alive. I'm finally learning that. I am truly finding happiness again. Yes, I still have my moments (do you blame me?) but overall, I'm doing great. Thriving and happy.

CONCLUSION

This is where I'm going to start wrapping things up. The tough part about this is the fact that I'm not writing a fictional novel- there's no clear beginning, middle, and end to my story. It's my life and I could honestly continue to write for a lifetime. For the longest time, I wanted to stop writing after my sister's wedding or after my last big surgery- but they just so happened to take place within four days of each other. There's so many other things that are happening in my life right now too. I could continue this book for the next ten years and even that wouldn't be enough. I'm not going to lie though, writing my thoughts, hopes, sadness, fears and laughs has been very hard but extremely therapeutic for me too. It's helped me understand and process my feelings better.

I don't know what my future has in store for me, but I do know that I'm one tough ass girl and I can face the world. I've gone to the abyss and back as Dr. Brady would say. I've gone through things in the last two years that some people will never face in their entire life, and I've been alright. Shit, I just wrote a whole book from my phone with my left thumb. I had five strokes, I was paralyzed, lost my voice, lost my smile, lost the ability to balance, lost my best friend in the world but here I am... still chugging along LOL. Can't get rid of me that quick.

Two and a half years ago, I know that any of those things would have completely broken me. But what happened to me has truly changed me as a human being. For the better. How I look at things is just different now- I have to be okay. I have no other choice but to be okay. I'll never let myself be a broken person. I've gone through major, major things without being broken. Nothing that I will ever face moving forward in my life could possibly be worse than what I've already faced in life. So I know that just about anything can be thrown at me and I will be fine. And that weirdly brings me peace. It's all about moving forward from here, not backwards.

I am still facing deficits that I hope will improve over time- my jaw, my balance, my eyes, my hand and my arm weakness. I'm honestly just trying to stay in a positive mindset though and trust God to do the rest. That's all that I can do. Obviously, I'm working hard and trying to improve what I can but I'm realizing that a lot of this recovery is just out of my hands. That was a tough pill for me to swallow at first but I've come to terms with it. Sometimes I feel as though there aren't enough hours in the day to work on rehabbing myself. My hand, my shoulder, my leg, my ankle, my face, my jaw, my eyes, my voice, my balance. 24 hours just isn't enough! But again, I'm looking to God to control what I can't. I know that things are just going to continue to get better.

I'm planning to get my first tattoo soon. I don't know when, but I've been thinking about it now for almost two years. I want a flower with the phrase "second chances" written on the stem to signify my brain stem. Second chances at literally everything. At first, I wanted to get a flower for every surgery that I've had, but at this point, I'd have a whole freaking bouquet of flowers on my arm. No thanks.

Since October, I've basically been living on my own, proving to myself that I can do this life all by myself. It's actually amazing to me that I can look at what I'm doing today and say that last year, I truly couldn't dream of living and doing things on my own. I was literally just getting comfortable with transferring from a wheelchair to the couch by myself. And the best part is that I keep getting better. And I will keep fighting to get better every single day for the rest of my life. I have nothing but life ahead of me- I'm still so young. I'm already able to see some positive changes in my face and it hasn't even been that long yet. I'm so looking forward to seeing even more changes as time goes on.

My plan for the new year is to move into an apartment by myself- maybe somewhere warm! Get a job, start driving again and get my service dog. I also want to open a small business with my sister too- we have a few ideas already in the works. Those are my major goals! A long term goal of mine is to open up my own coffee shop.

I just keep picturing the future in my head- being in my own place with my cute little service pup, my face is back to normal and I can walk around. I'm cleaning, cooking, doing laundry, working from home and driving myself around wherever I want, whenever I want. Ahhhh, independence. Those were all things that I took for granted that I am now looking forward to in my future. It makes me really excited. In my future, I also want to figure out how I can somehow connect young people who are in the same boat as me. It can be really therapeutic to talk to other people that can directly relate to me.

I connect with others on social media a lot. It's really inspiring for me. It also helps me because some of the people who follow me have privately messaged me and told me what my words do for them. Being able to help people cope through their situations is therapy for me. I just want to help people to do good and be good. To be grateful, have compassion, and understand that you can't always understand what it's like to be in someone else's shoes. But that's okay- reminding others to be kind to strangers. People fight visible and invisible battles everyday.

I feel like the second chance that God gave me is for a reason that I don't know just yet. I have my whole life ahead of me to find out.

ABOUT THE AUTHOR

Born and raised in New Jersey, Rachel Paverman graduated from Montclair State University with a BS in sports, events, and tourism marketing. She is inspired by hearing other people's stories and wants to share her own. One of her greatest motivations is getting better for those who were not granted the chance to. Rachel's hobbies include exercising, DIYing, cooking, watching New York Giant football, volunteering, and exploring the Jersey shore for the best coffee shops and beaches.